From GLORY to GLORY

Great beauty in seasons of pain
Strong at the broken places

From Glory to Glory

Great beauty in seasons of pain

Strong at the broken places

This publication is designed to provide competent and reliable information regarding the subject matter covered. The scanning, uploading, and distribution of this book without prior consent is a theft of the Author's Intellectual Property.

Unless otherwise indicated, Scripture quotations are taken mainly from the HOLY BIBLE, NEW INTERNATIONAL VERSION (NIV). Other versions apply including AMP, KJV, and NKJV.

Blog: www.womansworthconference.wordpress.com

W: www.authenticworth.com

E: authenticworth@gmail.com

YouTube Channel: Esther N J

ISBN NUMBER: 978-1-9160600-0-5

In loving memory of my eldest and first dear sister, Glory Chidinma Jacob who was born on Monday 26th September 1983 and laid to rest on Friday 11th May 2018 at 07.00am - St Thomas' Hospital, Westminster, London, aged 34.

Dedicated to a precious unique sister, daughter, friend, and work colleague, Glory Chidinma Jacob. Your presence lives within our hearts. Nothing will replace you; from the day God created you till departure, a strong place in my heart you belong. God took you at His appointed time and left your father, mother and siblings here. Until we meet again I vow to always live a fruitful and fulfilling life, to inspire those around me and those I am due to know in the near future, to encourage and excel beyond the world's expectations. I know you would have been here to celebrate this third book, but I know your spirit already dwells within us. Keep on rejoicing. I will make you proud big sis! Dedicated to you, Glory!

--- ACKNOWLEDGEMENTS ---

Give honour to whom honour is due. Before I start, let me admire God Almighty; the One who has gifted me to write a third book. It takes a lot of sacrifice, consistency and time to write and feel led to inspire, motivate, influence, and transform the mind of the reader to cherish and appreciate life. The responses, feedback, and reviews from my previous books*: It's Time to Heal* and *Completion* have been humbling. This is not an opportunity I take lightly and look forward to where the writing career will take me.

My sincere gratitude goes to my special family; in particular, my wonderful parents, Justin & Patience Jacob for the way they have pushed, encouraged and prayed over my life from a young age, supporting me in business, personal and professional endeavours. I am also grateful for their continuous support on this project, always believing the best and interceding for me. They have both contributed *greatly* and I look forward to blessing you both for all you have bestowed on my life.

To my late first and eldest beautiful sister, Glory Chidinma Jacob, I salute you. My love for you is more than words can express! To my second eldest sister, Ruth Jacob and my brother Nathaniel-Faith Jacob, thank you both for supporting the vision and not doubting what I do. Without you all, it would have not been possible to be where I am today.

A special thanks to my website designer, Ali West, and logo designer, Matt Sykes, who have supported my vision in such a short amount of time, creating the website and logo for Authentic Worth. I met these lovely people in 2018 and they have truly gone beyond my expectations. For more information, visit the website on www.authenticworth.com.

My lovely friends, I call sisters, thank you and all those who have supported me along the way; those I have known for a length of time or just recently. You have believed in my vision, kept me strong and for being my biggest supporters. It has been a journey and I love the fact that the encouragement is always consistent, pushing me to be the best version of myself.

Pastor, Rev. Dr. Steve Armah, I salute and thank you for the times you allow me to use my home church, Sureway, to host my book launches; God will repay you. The support you have also given to the church, and helping it be what it is today is humbling.

Lastly, for all the social networking events I've attended in 2018, they have been extremely useful. The wisdom, knowledge, humour and rich content behind all that was presented has left me empowered and I look forward to attending many more events in the future and meet with like-minded future leaders.

Thank you to those I have met in 2019; the friendships and relationships built, I am grateful. Everyone that has contributed and supported this book will not be forgotten. Above all, I am thankful for the gift of writing and will use it to inspire many. Changing one life at a time as I am called for such a time as this. {Esther 4:14}.

--- CONTENTS ---

--- INTRODUCTION ---

--- G-L-O-R-Y! ---

Power – Authority – Strength – Praise – Honour – Riches – Respect

G L O R Y – God's character reveals His Glory. *Glory is expensive* – The Glory of God is in a class by Himself. He has infinite perfections, infinite greatness, and infinite worth. Powerful, yet invisible, He is perfect in all of His ways. He is the Master of the Universe. He is the ultimate chain breaker!

The greater the light in a dark room, the clearer it will be to walk in greatness. We were not made to dwell alone but go into a dark world and inspire. The Glory of God has to dwell within us for others to see our light.

Apostle Paul said, "Let your light shine out of darkness. His light shines in our hearts to give us the knowledge of God's Glory displayed in the face of Christ."

2 Corinthians 4:6

Be intentional about your impact on others. Our purpose leads to destiny and ensures that time lived isn't wasted because you don't know who is inspired by your journey.

The Glory of God, according to John Piper is:

"the infinite beauty and greatness of God's manifold perfections. His attributes and greatness are far too supreme to understand"

I am in admiration on all that God is doing, not just for the future but also what He did in the past that made me the woman I am right now.

Exodus 33:18-23 shows that while there are aspects of God's nature revealed to Moses, there are other aspects that are not revealed, including His face, meaning His Glory that can't be seen. We honour Him because we can't physically see Him, but His presence is very close which makes us aware of the Holy Spirit who is our Comforter in time of need.

There must be respect and honour in recognising the Glory of God. He is the definition of praise and authority. ***Glory can also be defined by someone moving on to Glory*** – for example, if a loved one has passed away, they have gone to Glory which is His Kingdom (heavenly home). It is much better than riches or wealth. From life's first cry to final breath we are assured that we have hope in the One who knows the end from the beginning.

Question(s):

What kind of Glory are you displaying towards those around you?

How is your light shining in other people lives?

Your words, actions, and thoughts play a massive role and as you continue this journey called life, use it to develop yourself and leave a legacy behind to those who need it. Let your life be authentic and ***make it count!***

--- CHAPTER 1 ---
The Comforter is Here

"Even though I walk through the valley of the shadow of death, I will fear no evil, for you are with me; your rod and your staff, they comfort me"

Psalm 23:4 (NIV)

Romans 8:28 (KJV):

"And we know that all things work out for the good of those who love the Lord; who are called according to His purpose"

How about when going through loss, emotional distress and isolation? We can still believe it is working for our utmost good. Our struggles give a new opportunity to test the anchor of our souls and in particular, when thoughts of anxiety and fear creep in, keeping us comfortable and complacent.

In my previous book, *Completion – From the Perspective of Brokenness*, I spoke about the beauty of being broken mentally and emotionally, and the importance of acknowledging the way our burdens make us whole. I never truly understood why I was broken, but it was God's role to comfort me and use the pain to transform into purpose for the benefit of other people.

Being able to understand the Will of God does not involve our opinion or what we think He should do on our behalf, or for our benefit. It is allowing Him to move thoroughly in the way He knows best, allowing His decisions to be above ours. It includes not being swayed by what we think we know, in comparison to what God already knows, because He knows our end from the beginning. This has honestly been one of the hardest challenges I've had to understand in 2018. It isn't always possible to obtain what we desire, especially when a specific timetable has been set for us to achieve it. However, there is always beauty in waiting for Him to step in. And with time, the pieces will all fit together to bring true and authentic wholeness. ***Do not take God for granted – take Him seriously at all times!***

The Holy Spirit knows us intimately. He knows our longings, our heart-language, and unspoken words and helps in our communication with Him.

Emotional Intelligence

Our feelings are here to stay. Sounds cliché, I know – but look deep within and ask yourself why you cry from time to time or feel that nobody understands you. I know how it feels to be misunderstood; you feel the need to justify yourself to others who may have a different perception of you. I've realised that some people are stronger at handling their feelings than others because they have disciplined their mental state to not go beyond their control; they have learnt how to master it through with the pressure that caused the dysfunction. On the contrary, there will always be an element of feeling comforted and wanting someone to understand how it feels to be in their shoes – this isn't a weakness; it is strength and a cry out for help in seasons of hopelessness. Do not undermine your tears or how someone made you cry the other night. If you think about it, it's helping you grow emotionally and mentally.

In my journey of wholeness, I've pretended that I was always happy, just to avoid internal conflict and make God smile, but why was I deceiving myself? I would look in the mirror and start to question whether I was happy, but deep down in my soul, I wasn't. There were plans I had in mind to fulfil by a certain age, and there were decisions I made for a better life that had not come to fruition; how could I pretend any longer? I didn't. I opened up to one or two people and decided to understand their perspective on life and how they handled their situations. Some understood me, others didn't and that was totally fine.

Your tears cleanse the soul – the more you keep it in, the more depressed you can become, and this can have an effect on your health and relationships with others. Release the pain, release the frustration, release the doubt and let your mind be FREE! Don't suppress the way you feel, no matter the situation. Feelings can be seen as good medicine to get rid of toxic thoughts and worrying minds that cause unnecessary tension.

I remember going to the *Called-Out Concert* on Saturday 10th November 2018 and one of my favourite worship singers, Phil Thompson, came with his band. He said something that was so profound, and I could not help but jot it down in my journal – *"our focus is too much on what happened in the past, or it is battling with what the unknown will look like in years to come, but how about just focusing on the present?"*

I held my hands so tight because it resonated with me very quickly! I am always thinking about what I could have done better and what I would want my future to look like. However, I have not even embraced the fact that I have already come far in the season I am currently, that I can motivate and congratulate myself for writing two books, opportunities to speak about my journey to other people and at events and having a website. You see, if we are not careful we will always worry about why things did not work out in our past or wishing that our future will come right now. Learn how to **celebrate the small steps rather than focusing on bigger blessings.** Your past and your future should not interfere with where you are right now unless it's to help you and build you into a better person. Your present is NOW, not yesterday or tomorrow.

We won't always have it together, and that is okay. When I look back over my life, I remember to thank God for all the blessings He did not give me when I wanted them, because I now know that I would not have been able to handle them. Do you remember those goals in your journal, notepad, your phone, the ones you were able to tick a few off, but realised the list had a long way to go?

Eventually, you start to feel discouraged and become lazy because of the delay, but what we don't always realise is that *getting everything at once can be difficult to handle.* It is easy to fall out of touch with our purpose and vision simply because the waiting game is long, but don't lose the determination. Do not allow the way you feel to make you forfeit and quit prematurely.

Failure, authenticity, and beauty are in the in-between stages of success, the lessons learnt along the journey, not just the final destination. The delays, pauses and long nights are teaching us something great – to keep on being determined to not give up. Nothing in life is going to be nourished until you invest and feed it.

The way you feel will not change your circumstances, but how you respond to it will.

In my early twenties, I was exposed to different kinds of emotions, and they led me to see how I was able to deal with my thought patterns - the way I would see my situation and how I would react to them. I was not the one to confront or make a scene. Over time, I learnt the importance of offering constructive criticism especially when it came to group activities or friendships. In my undergraduate degree, I was placed to work with people who had opposite personalities and different ways of learning. It was then that I realised that we are all unique and have our own style of working.

Emotions and our inner-spirit will always be in conflict and these two forces are a way to either get you to surrender to God or suppress and deal with it yourself. In essence, it is helpful to know the importance of feelings, so you can fight more effectively when they unexpectedly come to mind.

Why do we ignore the way we feel, you may ask? There must be some Glory in our tears. Of COURSE, there is!

For me, personally, I have prayed with utter strength, and I have also prayed with tears

I don't know about you, but there is something that brings God's immediate attention when you cry. The Heavens roar when He sees the tears that fall from our eyes. When I have no words to say, all I can do is cry, and this is me being real. This is not to say that I can't pray, or I don't trust His ways, but when pain is unbearable, what words can you utter?

As I was studying, I thought of researching the different ways that feelings impact our minds and daily living. We can all fall into the following categories when handling how we feel. Some are more sensitive than others, but I know you can relate to the following:

> - **Anger** – Psalm 37:8 (NIV) – "Refrain from anger and turn from wrath; do not fret – it leads only to evil."

> - **Affection** – Songs of Solomon 8:4 (NIV) – "Daughters of Jerusalem, I charge you: Do not arouse or awaken love until it so desires."

> - **Delight** – Psalm 37:4 (NIV) – "Delight yourself in the Lord, and He will give you the desires of your heart."

> - **Fear** – Luke 12:5 (NIV) – "But I will show you whom you should fear: Fear Him who, after the killing of the body, has power to throw you into hell. Yes, I tell you, fear Him."

> - **Joy** – Psalm 5:11 (NIV) – "But let all who take refuge in you be glad; let them ever sing for joy. Spread your protection over them, that those who love your name may rejoice in you."

These scriptures indicate what our hearts love, trust and fear. Our feelings will tap into these areas in times of trouble, but they should also be used as a source of encouragement. To expand further:

Anger - there is positive and negative anger. There is anger that can be good, such as when a child is being disciplined for inappropriate behaviour. However, there is another anger that shows no mercy and an uncontrolled spirit which causes one to operate in regretful ways.

For example, speaking negative words over your children - words have power! Do not go to the extent where you question your existence because you lack self-control to handle emotions. Fear is used with wisdom and balance, not out of proportion.

Affection – the way we feel about someone will present a lot of affection, whether physically or emotionally. I honestly love the way King Solomon admires his lover in Songs of Solomon chapter 7. You will see that he mentioned in verse 6 how beautiful and pleasing she is. It is an honour to get compliments from time to time; it makes you feel valued. It is vital for a man and woman to be romantic and express the way they feel. Love is a beautiful thing!

Delight – in anything you do, put all your effort into it. To add to this, I recall Proverbs 16:3 which declares that you should:

"Commit to the Lord whatever you do, and your plans will succeed"

I remember a friend told me to read this scripture as I was in my exam season for third year at university. I used this scripture all the time before I started to revise and felt convinced that my work would be successful. Indeed, it was, and I achieved a 2:1. I believe in everything we do, we must put in the work and take pleasure in the tasks that are being given to us. To wrap it up, be intentional about what you want to achieve. Let your investment be so great that when you see the return, you will truly understand the importance of being in a season of delight. Happiness and joy follow on from this.

Fear – why do we fear? It is because we can't see the other side. This causes so much anxiety and I have been in positions where fear has made me stagnant; not knowing what to do or where to turn. In these types of situations, choose to take authority over fear and use it as a tool to ignite your faith. *Fear and faith can't live in the same room*, one must outdo the other, and I choose FAITH! In some cases, some of us mistake standing still for doing nothing, which is why fear creeps in. FEAR says 'DO SOMETHING QUICKLY' and FAITH says 'STAND STILL IN FAITH'. Can you see the difference? If you move with fear, you will not get far and mistakenly rush the process, meaning you will have to start from the beginning again.

Joy – when there is joy inside of you there is peace externally. Ask yourself whether you are happy right now – this is the best way to appreciate how far you have come, rather than focusing on past failures. This is just unnecessary pressure causing a flow of low self-esteem to germinate within. It is important to be thankful for at least one thing that has happened, for example, you are alive and well, reading this book. Joy also enables you to have emotional stability.

In essence, Peter Salavoy and John Mayer (2018) defined emotional intelligence as:

"The ability to understand, manage and influence the emotions of others and ourselves"

The points emphasised above suggest that we apply them to ourselves as well as others in a mature manner. I remember speaking with a friend about sympathy and empathy. We were more closely related to empathy as we spoke about the dramatic impact social media is currently having on teenagers and young adults. It is easy to sympathise with someone who is going through financial struggles, but when it comes to losing a family friend or loved one, empathy has to be much greater. When you have someone who can cry with you, it is a blessing.

I remember the way my friend was speaking; what he was going through wasn't giving him peace of mind. I could sympathise with him, because although I couldn't relate to his situation, I understood where he was coming from. If you do not know how to help someone in their time of need and have not been through what they have encountered, be silent and just listen. People do not need to be lectured, telling them what to do and what not to do. This is something that I am learning also. It can be easy to bring your own methods and past experiences into how you dealt with a situation, but from the other person's perspective, it won't always be easy to understand.

On one occasion I took my parents' home after church, and my dad was watching a video about a man who went through a hard time in his childhood. I can't remember his name, but now he is a motivational speaker. He would speak about how his father mistreated him at home and how he didn't eat for days. One thing which stood out to me was when the man mentioned that his father beat him with a thick belt that stripped off his flesh, and how it took him a very long time to forgive him. The healing process took months, and he could not understand why a biological father would do this to him.

He subsequently abused relationships with friends and loved ones and blamed his behaviour on the fact that he was harshly punished by his father. As they did not understand all that he went through in his past, he lost many friends because of this. The one cautionary statement the man made was this: "anytime you speak to someone or try to get their attention and they retaliate in a harsh manner, do not take it to heart; you do not know what they had to put up with in their past"

How many times have we taken a genuine approach towards people only for them to be disrespectful, without understanding their story? You have no clue what the person next to you, even your closest friend is going through for that reaction to occur. As painful as it may sound, the best way to understand one's situation is trying not to take offence. Offence builds tension in your heart, in your mind and in your health. The friction you have with one person can affect the way you perceive others. This should not be so. Do I blame the man who said the statement? Of course not, but what he did not realise was the Glory that was attached to his story that made him be the man he is today. He now uses his story to share with hurting people who feel abused, misunderstood and broken around the world.

When we struggle with situations, do not see it as a type of punishment. It is an opportunity to come out of the pity-party comfort zone and help the person who is going through the same issue. For the person who may want to commit suicide or the mother who wants to give up looking after her child, your pain is not meant to be for you alone. God is going to get Glory from your situation. Allow Him to be God over your life. It is also encouraging to know that you don't need to chase what God sends your way. Whether there is pain in your life, learn to handle it well, with maturity and ease. Life will always have its ups and downs, but it is about understanding that God will never give up on us as long as we do not give up on Him. He is giving us the strength to face each day as it comes.

The Holy Spirit is a Comforter

Through all you have been through, God is going to get Glory out of it. He would not bring you this far just to leave you, He would not make a way if He didn't care. He wouldn't have given His life if He didn't love you. He wouldn't lift you up to let you down.

Some go to palm-readers to ease their mind, but I know a true and real Comforter who is *free of charge* and knows everything about my life. The Holy Spirit is so gentle, it is revealed to those that seek Him. It intervenes when you have no words to say. I remember speaking to a dear sister and mentioned that *surrender* has been one of the tools that caused her to fulfil her purpose. This is something that I've learnt in 2018, not trying to pick up the issue and sort it out by myself, knowing that it will cause potential damage. How many of us have the tendency to always be in control of everything?

When you are surrounded by people who are achieving their goals and desires, your intentions and determination become twice as strong, because you know that what is invested can come out and produce twice as much. Believe me, however, it is HARD WORK! Don't take it for granted and sit down thinking it will be easy; nothing that is going to be impactful is going to be easy, but that is what makes it worth investing in at the initial stages. By faith, YES it will be easy, but faith without works is dead. We can keep talking but are we taking action?

From Glory to Glory

Following the crowd looks good, but we must have a vision and good intent in mind of where we are going, not to follow the crowd because you are bored. If you do not know why you are doing something, do not make a decision in haste; you must have a vision or purpose with the next phase of your life. Do not feel the need to copy others either because where they are going may not be your route. You can learn and be inspired, but do not let the pressure of involving yourself in a project become a burden. This is why it is important that the Holy Spirit is involved to teach, comfort and lead us. In 2018 my faith grew drastically, because of all the things that happened which I will explain in Chapters 5 and 6. It has taught me to know what to focus on, how the vision for my life is to be taken seriously, and more importantly, to be thankful for the gift of life.

There will be a time where you need to practice being still at the expense of not always hearing God speak. Remember that your tears are God's way of saying He has heard you, so if they need to fall out, let them do so. I strongly agree that you will be in a much better place if you release what is causing you frustration. As I mentioned in my video on YouTube about Mental Health, your tears are not just for you but to help the next person who is going through their own struggle.

I took a week off work and social media in September 2018 to have *me* time. I strongly advise for those who work to take time off and invest in you. Work on your health, your mind, your thoughts and life. This takes consistent practise, and each day you will learn something different, that you may not have learnt if you were in a comfortable environment.

Everyday life teaches and reveals something new, but only if you allow yourself to have a day of rest. I read a two-month booklet called *Every Day with Jesus*. One of the months, September, really stood out for me as it focused on how we should keep the Sabbath Day holy. The Sabbath Day is mainly known to be held on a Saturday, however, I am aware that some Christians go to church on Sundays. I do attend church on Sundays and I know that is meant to be a day of rest, but can I be honest with you? At times, I still do work - lol! I feel there is no day off, but once my body tells me to rest, I will.

It is important to give yourself at least one day in the week to reflect, relax and take a break. Don't do too much at the expense of your well-being. It is vital to take rest, so you can give your mind ease to prepare for the week ahead. When this happens, you are able to plan your day one step at a time. Allowing yourself to focus on too much at one time is detrimental and can cause dysfunction with family and friends, and key worth relationships with others.

I remember when it felt as if I did not have enough time for myself, and that was because I was too focused on being present for other people. People are important, but so are YOU! Don't forget that. Where there is balance, there is peace. Being able to look after you and others is very important, but don't overdo it where you take on too much. It is vital to get to a stage where you are able to block out the voices of people and submit to the Holy Spirit so that He can speak; even when He is silent, do not confuse that with His sovereignty and what He can do.

There will be seasons of surrendering in order to increase our faith levels, rather than trying to prove to the Holy Spirit that we can do everything and assuming He will catch up. The Holy Spirit doesn't want the remaining pieces, He wants all of you: the confusion, the brokenness, the pain, the worry, the fear, the anxiety.

To top that, do you realise that you will never be alone in life? Even though it may feel like it, the right people will come in your life at the appointed time. When you meet with people, it will align you to the purpose that is in you to fulfil purpose. *Life will catch up with you and it will be such a dramatic change that you won't even begin to understand how you got there.* And it was all because you 'SURRENDERED'. This word has got me so excited - not to say I won't work hard, no that is not what I am saying, but to do the best you can and WAIT expectantly for the Holy Spirit to move on your behalf will greatly honour Him.

The Holy Spirit is real. I do not have enough words that can fully articulate that fact. Going home from dinner at Oxford Street with my friend, I recall my train at Lewisham Station. As I arrived at the station, I saw a train afar off thinking that it arrived, not realising that it was on the other side of the platform. As I saw it, what did my mind do? It went into doubt-mode. I concluded I'd have to wait 20 minutes for the next one to come, plus it was too cold! As I approached the station, I realised my train had literally just arrived. I was so happy! The Holy Spirit prompted me and realised that worrying was simply for nothing. For those who worry about minor things, don't allow them to get the best of you.

When I reached home, I just laughed and asked myself why I was so doubtful in the first place. Yes, I know transport isn't always reliable, but there must be understanding: what if the train you wanted to take was delayed because a fire occurred fifteen minutes away from your station? Or how about a broken track that caused passengers to stay on the train for more than two hours! You just never know, and this was why the Holy Spirit encouraged me that night not to worry about delays. Some delays are very good, so before you doubt, ask what you need to learn because every delay has a lesson behind it.

The question for us to consider is, can God trust us in seeking after His heart, or are we only out for God's hand? We should not just serve God for what is in His hand, but also, who He is to us. From a Biblical perspective, King Saul wanted the position and not the presence (1 Samuel 15). Imagine only seeking the Holy Spirit when you are in need and not having an encounter with Him for who He is. I have been convinced that through the intention of our hearts in seeking God for who He is, and not only what He has done, it grants us more access into His presence and enables us to gain deeper strength in our personal lives. Let this be a constant reminder.

God Understands

The title says it all – what is there not to understand! The attributes that God carries is of a loving and understanding nature. A loving person will always understand the way you feel, especially when it hurts the most; someone who can sympathise and empathise with you is priceless. You can't love someone you do not understand, right? Of course not, which is why communication, honesty, and transparency are key aspects to building a strong relationship.

In essence, there must be discipline when speaking and the other person listens. It can't be two people talking at the same time. Where is the respect? Where is the honour? There has to be a mutual agreement of understanding what the other person is saying, before speaking. I remember listening to the news at one point and there were three guests who were invited to speak about a topic.

I was talking to my sister about this, trying to understand why they were all speaking at once and could hardly hear what they were saying. In life, there is a tendency to get our voices heard, but wouldn't it be wise to allow one person to speak first, and the other listen? Even today, it happens! We listen to reply/respond, but we must learn to listen and take into account what is being said, to then give a wise response.

You are honouring the person by showing respect. This is how it is with God. When He speaks, we must tune our ears to listen attentively. We all have a story and I know we want to be heard, but when it does not happen how do you react? Who can you turn to for your mind to be at ease? God is the greatest listener – in my previous book, *Completion*, I mentioned that the tears soaking your pillow are great signs that God understands what you are going through. There will be days where you won't be able to talk, it is your tears that do the talking, but He understands. I remember someone saying to me that when you want something so badly, the first time you mentioned that need, God heard. And it is true till today. God is hearing you and always will, but also learn how to wait for Him to speak.

From Glory to Glory

I have understood why people tend to misinterpret the power of God or underestimate who He is because they have not come to the point where they want to understand Him; this could be due to impatience or lack of understanding of who He is and how He operates. To add, some have not given God the chance to come into their lives and see what He can do. His power and existence can't be understood because *He is indescribable*. When I say God understands the pain you go through, He really does. It may not seem like it because why would a good God allow painful situations to occur? You may be wondering about this, and I totally understand your thoughts. But how about being able to understand that this could be an opportunity for God to show Himself strong in that situation you are facing?

The way I see it, God loves to show off, in particular, His power in order for our lives to be better. I know it may be hard to digest, especially due to what the past has presented itself to be. However, without any problems, how would we acknowledge that there really is a God? If everything went well according to your plan, would you appreciate or thank Him?

On the contrary, perhaps people's expectations are weighing you down. The pressure can mount up because we are conscious of what people expect of us. But what do you do when you are not understood by family or friends? What if you made a decision that people around you would think you've gone out of your mind? To leave a full-time job that pays well to travel and start a new life, or to start a business with low capital - it takes strength to make a decision like this, but only take it when God leads you.

We genuinely need people who can dedicate their time to work nine to five each day; if everyone was self-employed, who would work with the transportation services, deliver and provide goods to supermarkets, take care of the sick etc. For those who may feel overwhelmed and frustrated, hold on; better is coming. Do not despise the job or season you are in; it is teaching and preparing you for greater things ahead.

I have learnt to do what enables me to grow effectively – following God's plan for my life with confidence, because He understands where

I am going, especially when I do not know which way to turn or start. *The experiences you encounter each day shape you for a better tomorrow.* Learn to count your blessings more than your problems and eventually you will become fully dependent on the One who knows you best. He will give you boldness, wisdom, confidence and more importantly, a heart to love.

Focus your mind on all that is going on around you at this present moment: God says, '*I am He that is*'. God is not just the Creator, but the One who reveals Himself to people. Understanding who God is and what He has done is essential to comprehending the reason for His goodness in our lives. Even when we feel challenged we are able to understand the deeper meaning behind it, because He knows all things. We do not need to be alarmed when something serious happens. We can also use our situations to inspire other people and help them, particularly those who are battling with mental health. Your mind and thoughts reveal a lot about the level of understanding you have in someone.

If your thoughts towards someone are not positive, you are most likely to have negative perceptions of the person. When I see something great about someone, it connects me to them. However, no matter how much I try to see the best in someone, especially if there has been a misunderstanding in the past, it can have its downfalls. It is a psychological-mutual feeling. It takes a strong mind to overlook what happened and give the person another chance to understand how they are feeling. We can empathise and think about the situation from another person's point of view.

Understanding is something I've had to come to terms with, especially when I thought I was able to figure out life, in my own strength. I have a positive and winning attitude, but the minute a thought would come in my mind, it would cause me to re-think - am I really making the right decision? Is anyone going to support my vision? Am I going to be doing this by myself? I did not realise that it was all due to different types of fear running in my head. I know we all go through this, I am not alone in this regard. We just want someone to understand what plans have been made and how to get there, and not be intimidated by anyone's success, because behind the scenes, no one knows how the work is being done.

Do not put yourself down or question who you are if people do not understand your vision. When you surrender to God and have great faith, that is when answers will come to fruition. It takes discipline to starve the fears and keep the goals active. Do not let anyone who doesn't understand you get in the way of your achievements. Doing the unusual is not easy, but it is so worth it.

One of the main characteristics I adore is when people fulfil their purpose and don't need to boast about what they have done for attention. It is not about showing everyone on social media that you have made it unless you are doing it to the Glory of God, because it is not about you in the first place. Later in the book, I'll be talking about the consequences of speaking too soon.

When working in silence, you learn a lot about yourself and keeps you focused on *purpose*. Other times, it feels as if nothing is happening because the focus is on other people and how far they are in life, not realising that being able to wake up to brush your teeth and have a shower is a blessing in itself. For the one who does not struggle when eating or doesn't find it difficult to walk, be grateful for it. Being understood is about appreciating the path God has taken you through and therefore allowing Him to move you from one area to another. This is what From *Glory to Glory* is about.

If you have to second-guess who God is, I'll tell you now, don't. He is the rewarder of those who diligently and consistently seek His face (Hebrews 11:6). I am not saying this because I was brought up in a Christian household because during the process, I did not understand what it meant to have a relationship with Jesus. It did not stick to me, as I would assume church being for adults only. Seeing consistent changes in our world every day, I am more convinced that God indeed is real and has such a big heart of love for all. This is what causes me to understand Him and inspires me to stay closer.

It is uncomfortable to love someone and them not loving you - you aren't feeling them, but they are feeling you; you then sense a strong uncomfortable conviction.

When you love someone, and they don't love you back the same way, it hurts doesn't it? At times we do this to God, only seeking Him when we are in need. Let this not be so, because the love He has for you is far greater than the love of anyone else. God understands the depths of your pain and wants to fill it with His peace, so allow Him - as TD Jakes espoused in his sermon entitled, *Go After God's Heart* (January 2019).

"You miss people, but you don't miss God?"

TD Jakes

Don't find Comfort in People

"God is our refuge and strength, an ever-present help in trouble"

Psalm 46:1 (NIV)

In as much as we need people to help us grow in life, we also need to have balance regarding our personal decisions. I encountered friendships that have been unfruitful, those that dropped in and out of my life. Have you noticed the more you try to save a friendship, the more damaging it can be to yourself? No matter what, we will have an opportunity to analyse those closest to us which is healthy.

As we grow, we become more aware of our strengths and weaknesses, as well as of those around us. I have been exposed to a few people who have tested my faith and love. Some I've had to let go of in humility, and others I've made an attempt to keep. There have been times I had to pray for God to remove me from anyone that may be subconsciously affected by my personality or character. It's a real humbling prayer, I tell you!

I remember a dear friend I thought would be a special part of my life - to understand that it had to end was not what I expected, but God knows best. You will know when something has to end due to the way you feel, act, and behave (especially your instinct). I've learnt not to suppress my feelings. Do not put yourself in trouble by trying to help everyone. When you fall out, pray about the situation. Let it all out and be free! The right people will be present at the right time.

> *Do not force friendships or relationships to ripen, especially when they are not ready.*

Everyone in your life is either there for a reason, a season, or a purpose/lifetime. But do not allow them to be your full source of strength. In my first book, *It's Time to Heal,* I remember talking about a friend who meant a lot to me but caused a lot of insecurities and had to re-take an exam in second year of university. I held this friendship very close because it felt like my only real friendship! To realise that it had to end caused me a lot of pain and tension.

I remember a period when my face was ridiculously spotty. I couldn't understand how the battles raging in my mind could affect my skin. Before, I'd blame myself why the friendship was unstable, but this did not matter. It was overdue and past its expiry date. Thank God I am strong at the broken places! *God had to come in and break the friendship before it would have broken me*. Now, I am at a stage where I understand the importance of friendships based on QUALITY and not QUANTITY or length of years. Don't let this be a mistake. You can know someone for twenty years, relative to someone for up to two years and has greater impact. Every day you learn key lessons that makes you wiser. My experiences with friends have truly made me stronger in God and myself.

We are all at different stages of life, but we learn most in pain

When you are in trouble, the first instinct would be to call a loved one, family member or friend. I just prefer to write how I feel in my journal and worship. It gives me strength that I would not have experienced had I opened up too quickly (thank God for past lessons!) Why is it that when we need help or assistance, we are quick to run to our best friend or loved one? As I am learning about the beauty of life, I understand the true importance of giving my undivided attention to God.

In order to function, we all inevitably look to something beyond ourselves – this is **worship**. It gives a set of values and priorities that guide us and influence our decisions – to fully surrender our burdens to God and let the focus be on Him and not on our circumstances. He is bigger than our problems! This, therefore, disciplines us not to always find comfort in people, but if it is so, God will use someone to speak at the time of need. He knows the right person to hook you up with, as long as you seek Him first (Matthew 6:33).

I remember speaking to a friend about his business and how he started, the successes and pitfalls. The first few words he said was *"DON'T LOOK BACK"*. *The smallest words can have the biggest impact.* This was not the first time I heard this, but it felt like a reoccurrence. I use these three words to inspire other people no matter what changes they make, not to look back. When I thought about this, I pictured God being the *centre of* everything; moving from depending on people to acknowledging God who knows every single hair on my head. I had to realise that my life was in transition and it was not comfortable. My dependence on those around me was distracting my full attention to honour and acknowledge God.

When you follow your own set of moral values without any reference to God, the worldly desires take over and become overwhelmed with what is happening on social media, which becomes difficult to seek His help. When I get too comfortable with certain people, it is easy to enjoy their company, but when my heart stays connected to the source (God), there is an aspect in me that automatically becomes dependent on Him – to be aware of the fact that God is jealous and wants us for His own, to have a rich, intimate relationship, trusting Him alone (my resource). As the saying goes 'you are who you hang around', so when you decide to make decisions, check your surroundings first.

As emphasised previously, Matthew 6:33 is about seeking God first. I am used to doing everything in my own strength and this has become a routine. When my heart is heavy, I need to pause and examine my mind. I do fail when doing this because I always want to be in control. Perhaps my way of doing things may be too ambitious but having the 'I know it all' mentality makes it difficult to fully depend on Him and draw grace and strength to live powerfully. It causes me to be comfortable, rather than speak to God about how I feel, I would go to the next person. Remember that it is not wrong to speak to people, but there must be a high honour for God to know all our problems and secret struggles *__first__*.

It becomes comfortable and yet tiring keeping people up to date with your life and having to keep it going for them to be interested or entertained. This is pressure. Why put yourself in this situation? Which reminds me to mention that speaking pre-maturely will make you have this lifestyle. When you speak too soon when something has not yet happened, you'll have to live up to the expectations of what people say and how they perceive you to be. This is dangerous and can cause you to double think who you are. Being indecisive is destroying our minds and causes us to be unstable, trying to change for people so they can like or approve of us. The pure reason as to why we shouldn't find comfort in people is because God wants you. He knows that the person you put your effort into will break your heart. Jeremiah 17:9 instructs us that:

"The heart is deceitful above all things and beyond cure; who can understand it?"

No matter how much we try to live a righteous life, there will always be flaws in us, but this should not be the definition of who we are. The question is, do you know who you are? Let's find out: In previous years having experienced various friendships and relationships, I have learnt the true importance of being complete in God. No matter how much I may want a family member or friend to understand me, they fully can't, and this does not mean they are not helpful; it shows that God is the only one who can satisfy our needs. There is always that person you would like to fully understand, but no one can understand us 100%. God did not create us to please everyone. You and I are fickle. We can only do so much, but GOD is unlimited!

A song that kept me going at university is *Nobody Greater* by VaShawn Mitchell. When listening to Gospel singers, I take every single word into account because it truly ministers to my heart. VaShawn starts off with the following lyrics:

"I climbed up to the highest mountain, looked all around, couldn't find nobody. Went down into the deepest valley, looked all around down there couldn't find nobody"

You will realise that not everybody will be around when you need them most, and this is where the Comforter comes in.

When my season feels dry, I am very specific on what I do; firstly, being able to seek closure with God. In the most painful season, God can be silent at times. Believe me, I know. I can try to run to everyone else, shop online as retail therapy, attend several events, but once I get home, I am responsible for my own emotions. I know what it is to find comfort in people and feeling worthless without them, not realising that all I had was already in me. I am complete through the Word of God.

If you lose yourself in the process of allowing God to make you into what He has ordained, you will eventually lose your power and invest in someone who may likely take advantage.

From Glory to Glory

When you are weak, going to others for comfort, who have their own problems, isn't always a suitable route. You must know who you are and when to speak about certain situations. Not everything has to be said. ***Do not play so many roles for people to like you.*** Know what gifts you bring to the table so there will be a level of respect. You should know who you are whether people believe in you or not. Don't wait for anyone to celebrate you; learn to celebrate yourself, not in a self-righteous way, but with humility and thanksgiving to God.

Although it can be seen that people's perception of you can have an impact on your performance, we must also be careful to make sure that what someone has sown in our minds doesn't control us. In other words, what someone thinks should not have power over you. What defines you is far greater than the words of others. You can't be accepting opinions of people and expect to upgrade on another level, although it is hard being surrounded by people who do not get you. Whether they understand you or not, you have to be willing to rise above the opinions and manage how to live in the midst of controversy.

From experience, I have shared my plans and hopes with friends and at times what I had in mind did not come to fruition. When they'd ask, 'Esther, how did it go, etc?' *awkward silence*. I then realised that God was secondary, and my friends were primary. They were my first source in my decisions. I am wiser and being even more careful of who I confide in and want to pass this on to you. Remember not everything has to be said prematurely; we should bring God into it first, and then others, if necessary. I learnt great lessons from speaking too soon and I am here to encourage you to learn from what I experienced.

Speaking prematurely without any substance is a potential danger to you and the vision. If God has not laid it on your heart to speak, then, by all means, keep it to yourself until revealed. I honour my friend who kept her engagement private, only to do a traditional wedding nine months later. We do not know who may be watching or who is around when speaking.

There is a saying that when someone speaks about you, it is not necessarily the way it has been said, but instead, they will never forget how it made them feel. You don't want to be carrying this burden of guilt around, so *learn to discipline your mouth before it disciplines you*. As my primary school teacher would say: 'If you do not have anything nice to say, please do not say anything at all.' Silence is expensive, so don't feel the need to talk anyhow to break the silence; instead, think before using your words.

Remember this: *if people get into your stronghold, they will get into your advantage*. People will have a 'strong hold' on you if you allow them to. There may be situations that you'll be able to let go of because of your dependency on God alone, however, there will be situations where it won't always be easy to shake off. This is why it is crucial to never depend on anyone 100% as mentioned before. Don't be attached to people that you can't function without their presence. Don't lose your focus because of negative strongholds.

If you are serious about experiencing the Glory of God in your life, get into His presence and you'll have complete peace. The things that used to bother you will no longer matter, simply because you've understood the importance of not finding comfort in people.

STRENGTH!

"You are my strength, strength like no other, strength like no other, reaches to me. In the fullness of Your Grace, in the Power of Your Name, You lift me up"

Madelyn Berry

Another favourite gospel song to date; the words speak volumes in times of weakness. When the mind plays with emotions, I would think about the good times I had with certain people, but then it would dawn on me that they were no longer around. I remember two dear friends in 2017 who I called sisters who weren't present life at a time when it was difficult. I thought they would stand by me but to no avail. In my first

25

book, It's Time to Heal, I examined the meaning of friendship in chapter 2.

For those who know me, I am a strong advocate in offering advice for authentic friendships because I know how important they are. TD Jakes mentioned in his friendship sermon that there are three types of friends who we will all encounter in life:

(1) Confidants – these are people who love you unconditionally, regardless of the situation or what happened in the past, present and future. They will stand with you.

(2) Constituencies – these are people who love you for what they can get from you. Be alert!

(3) Comrades – these are people who do not have your best interest at heart. Open your eyes.

I remember crying and writing at the same time because the feeling of being used isn't cute! We need pure, true and long-term friendships; however, it takes time to build. Please note: when the goals and visions you set come to fruition, you will start to realise a shift in friendships. When things look uncertain, God is protecting you from someone who may potentially harm your destiny, knowing that the friendship line has ended.

As you grow, God starts shaking certain people around, but do not worry, it is all working out for your good (Romans 8:28). To me, I did not understand why people I loved were leaving, however, I can look back and say how thankful I am for the strength God gave me to accept it and move on with ease. This truly made me stronger. More importantly, it brought me much closer to God.

True knowledge of Me comes when I am valued

God

Anything you find useful you will value, right? To place **ME** above everything else in life is unhelpful to your growth. We can't always understand the way God works, but there is peace of mind when we value and appreciate His sovereignty. Of course, it is not easy being in the waiting room, but you learn so much where you mature and grow into a deeper understanding of the way He works.

Can I ask who are you depending on to comfort you right now? Who are you giving your time, energy and tears to regarding that painful situation? Perhaps the man who disrespected you in the past, or the friend who didn't support your goals. I recall the story of Samson and Delilah in Judges 16:4 (NIV). Samson fell in love with a woman in the Valley of Sorek; her name was Delilah. The rulers of the Philistines spoke to Delilah and asked if she could find out Samson's secret behind his strength, so they could take it and overpower him because he was too strong for them. Had she successfully completed the assignment, she would receive eleven hundred shekels of silver.

Following on in verse 17 (NIV), Samson said:

"No razor has ever been used on my head because I have been a Nazirite dedicated to God from my mother's womb. If my head were shaved, my strength would leave me, and I would become as weak as any other man"

In verse 19, whilst Samson lay his head on Delilah, he went into a deep sleep. Delilah had then shaved off the seven braids of his hair, and eventually, Samson's strength started to leave him. Samson eventually woke up and as soon as Delilah announced the Philistines were pursuing him, Samson tried to escape but he couldn't, not realising that the Lord had left him, and the Philistines removed his eyes *(For your sanity: be careful where you lay your head – in other words, be discerning who you confide in!)*

This story teaches to know your surroundings. I am in awe that towards the end, although Samson could not see, God still gave him the strength to conquer the Philistines by pushing the Pillars where they were gathering, and it fell on all of them. Do not be quick to speak about your weaknesses, especially if you have not healed from them. We all have weaknesses and handle them differently, but it should not be a gateway for people to have easy access to them. Do not allow this to be you.

The legacy we leave matters more than what other people think. Each day has its struggles but God being all-knowing will empower us with the strength and knowledge to keep going. How do you deal with pain when you are weak? For me, it is being in God's presence as that is where I am able to engage in deep reflection. I can be real about EVERYTHING! I can't handle my battles alone. Jealous and envious thoughts run through all of our minds; this is something that isn't always easy to avoid. However, in expressing gratitude, it strengthens our mind-sets to see life from a positive place.

2018 taught me is to invest in inner-strength.

I want to encourage you to keep building yourself and the vision. The struggles and effort will build, transform and strengthen your resolve to keep going. You may have the desire to set up a business, but not enough experience. Do not disqualify yourself because you have what it takes! Do not wait in expectation but take action. It is very important that when you are choosing your next business partner or opportunity, discipline yourself to listen first then speak if necessary. Don't speak out of proportion but take key tips from discussions and use it wisely.

Strength is coming out of your comfort zone. When you are in a place of growth, it will cause you to become uncomfortable to the extent where you outgrow what you consider to be normal. It involves risks because if there is no risk, there will be no reward. For each risk that one takes, there is a reward stored up. If you want to see the reward, keep doing things you've never done before.

Easy to understand, yet difficult to do because complacency becomes your comfort. Strength takes place in the form of risk – yes, it feels uncertain but that is the beauty of it. You can't expect to be a millionaire if you have uncontrollable spending habits. Change your strategy. Shake it up a little! Do something uniquely crazy! If you do not give up, it will work for you!

July 2018 - The Big Debate! For those who know me, they will know I always have annual events every July. Due to the heavy responses regarding how I started my book journey, I decided to have my first book workshop for beginners in November 2018 and continued a second session in February 2019. Sometimes, you will be exposed to doing things you may feel unqualified for, but when you start, you'll realise that everything was already in you.

Remember this: you don't have to be great to get started; you just have to start in order to be great.

Strength is attractive, and this is what makes others be inspired. It is about being your authentic self, using your pain and turning it into purpose. This is how you are able to establish yourself and create a pathway for others to be strengthened through your testimony. I am encouraged by listening to preachers including my Pastor, Rev. Dr. Steve Armah, Bishop TD Jakes, Sarah Jakes, Steven Furtick, Joyce Meyer, to name a few, because they have all been on a journey; a journey of strength to continue the road ahead. Who said it was going to be easy? The journey won't always be easy, but it will add value to someone else, so let your life be meaningful, purposeful and transformative.

Remember that what you magnify will become bigger, so it is vital to discipline your thoughts at all times. "When praises go up, blessings come down". I can't believe how powerful this statement is, because it is easy to be fixated on the problem. However, I must say that from experience, my best miracles and breakthroughs have been through praise and positive words of affirmation.

From Glory to Glory

Yes, there is so much noise, pressure, fear, and temptation, but you have what it takes to be an overcomer because greater is He that is in you than he that is in the world (1 John 4:4). I am not saying attacks won't come but be prepared for *when* they will arrive. I am learning that no matter what I go through, my story is used to inspire other people to grow and get better through it. We all have something to do; not to only exist but make an impact.

2018 has left me with the strength to pass on and I am believing that as you read this book, you will understand what my journey is about and how I use it to uplift, inspire, influence and transform the lives of many who are yet to know their identity.

Acknowledging weakness is a doorway to experiencing God's strength. Don't hide your flaws and pretend. Suppressing only intensifies the pain. Everybody is on a different journey, but how you handle your own journey makes the difference. Remember, the first thing the enemy wants to do when he attacks you is to shut your mouth, so don't allow it. When you open your mouth and use words wisely, strength is stirred up within - that disrupts the silence over your life so take action!

--- CHAPTER 2 ---
Worry is not your friend

"Trust in the Lord with all your heart and lean not on your own understanding (6) In all your ways acknowledge Him, and He will make your paths straight"

Proverbs 3: 5-6 (NIV)

You Need to Surrender

It is our choices that show what we truly are, far more than our abilities can fathom. The more we surrender to Jesus, the more He is able to give to us. Do you know that the more we hold a fraction of our problems, the more we are increasing them? How do you cope with loss? How do you react, and how do you encourage yourself in the healing process? Not having to know how everything should go in your life is a good thing. Imagine trying to figure out everything at once – it is too overwhelming. Believe me, I have been there. It is pressure to keep up with different thoughts, so don't give yourself brain-overload!

1 Peter 5:7 (NIV) teaches us to:

"CAST (lay down) all our anxiety on Him because He cares for us"

How amazing is this! Let this be in your mind constantly – imagine carrying two loads of heavy baggage weighing you down. You are tired, grumpy, frustrated, annoyed, and at times you are tempted to take it out on others. This is what you are carrying all around on your journey; it could be the baggage of unforgiveness, the baggage of bitterness, the baggage of low self-esteem. The journey is long enough, yet you still choose to carry that load. All these rob us of our next move in life and this should not be so.

Surrendering is not trying to fix problems in your own strength. I have been through my own fair share of trials which have given me no option but to surrender. I will bring you back to a time in February 2018 when I had to do a Speed Awareness Course for driving. I remember that

From Glory to Glory

Saturday evening dropping my friend and her two kids home, two sharp flashlights took me by surprise. When I say I was shocked, I really was, because in my heart I assumed I went just before amber. It informed that I went past the red traffic light! That being my first time, I didn't know what to expect. The camera had taken photos of my front and rear license plates.

Two weeks later the letter arrived at the doorpost. So many thoughts ran through my mind about what would happen next, such as whether I'd get three points on the license and have to pay a penalty fine. In my mind I knew there was no need to make room for worry as the deed had already been done. I chose to surrender.

A few months later, I walked into the exam room thinking I was going to do another driving test. To my surprise, it was only to sit down attentively and listen to what the teacher had to say about safety of driving, including speed on the roads. There were around thirty adults in the class, which also was a shock! I've never been in such an environment before. The result? I PASSED! I could not believe all that time I only had to leave it in God's hands. I could have thought of so many excuses not to attend but chose to go because I knew God was with me. No matter how small our prayer may be, God answers and knows them all.

As I mentioned earlier, our tears remind us that when we don't have the words to say, He understands and will answer us in ways unimaginable. For those who really know me, they see me as someone who is determined, hardworking and deeply focused. Why would I pay £91.00 to then doubt and worry? (that isn't cheap!) I did not want to see myself doing the test again and that was my promise to myself! If there is no belief, what else can you really achieve?

It is hard to do miracles where there is no belief!

How deep is this statement? Without faith, it is impossible to please God. We surrender our sickness, our troubled minds and our finances. Every time I worry about something, in order for me to go into the next phase, I discipline my mind to shake off the worry and fear the situation caused me. When I feel stagnant and can't move forward, I know there is something trying to pull me back to that comfortable spot. Eventually fear and comparison creep in which causes us to become uncomfortable and makes it hard to cultivate healthy relationships.

There is always a false sense of pride – it is sneaky and deceptive and teaches us to fight in our own strength, not needing anyone to help or support. This is what the enemy uses to mess with our minds which makes us accountable to how we feel, not realising that the cure to dealing with the problem is seeking God. We seek creation, but not the Creator of the universe. Pride can also be hidden in ways where we choose not to surrender. I genuinely did not know this until my friend was reading John Bevere's book, The Bait of Satan (2010). I have not read it yet, but what was said seemed so profound.

Not being able to address a situation is a form of pride; meaning that everything is all in your hands. Pride is an enmity to God because nothing should be above Him. There has to be respect, whether you are right or wrong in any situation, let pride come down. Pride should not be used to suppress anyone but to have humble pride is where you see yourself in high standard because the Holy One dwells in you.

We can't control life, neither can we control death but as long as we have today, that is what we can control.

Each day is an opportunity to write down the goals and be determined to work on them. The motive behind every accomplishment is important as we will see in Chapter 3. Our accomplishments should inspire other people to do well; it shouldn't just be for our own good.

From Glory to Glory

I held a workshop in November 2018 for those who were looking to write their first book. The few words I mentioned to the attendants was the power of their story making impact. People will only invest in something they are familiar with or have experienced and can relate to. You must learn to offer a solution to someone's need because that is what will give you the Unique Selling Point (USP). What makes you stand out from your competitors? The name of your business may sound powerful, but it must also be clear and concise; it must reinforce your products and services.

During my writing career, I decided to launch a website which is live. For more information, visit www.authenticworth.com. Authentic Worth is an online platform for men and women to know their true worth and have a tangible impact on our world through their story. This is how I started the vision of writing books through my blog in 2014, to creating the Authentic Worth website. Authentic Worth provides online masterclass courses on how to write a book, as well as proofreading & editing services which launched in May 2019.

I decided to connect my blog to the website as I wanted to continue the journey of inspiring and transforming lives. Did I have fears? Of course, I did. It takes a lot of great faith to step out of our comfort zone and do something completely different. I still remember someone I spoke to about corporate sponsors and when the person looked at my website and saw a scripture quote (Jeremiah 29:11), the person said that it would take away the interest of potential shareholders and sponsors investing in the business.

I had to think deep and question whether I wanted to take the scripture off the website. I made a decision not to, as I would not have been my authentic self. Just to sign a contract I had to do what others told me would be suitable but, in my heart, I stand on the Word of God, so I decided to have a brief chat with my mother. Humbled by her feedback, I realise that people only want quick results for their own benefit but no impact towards other people. This is the world we are living in. Just 'change' so you can be one of us; 'if you want to get rich quicker, take this approach,' etc. I fully came to the understanding that not everyone will agree with my vision, but what matters is that I stay true to myself. No matter what you do, the truth will eventually come out and people will see what you stand for. It's important to stay true to who you are, rather than please people. This is Authentic Worth represents.

In my previous role, a lady who worked evening shifts came up to me, surprisingly, and mentioned that she didn't know I had written a book. I nodded. She was so intrigued, and we had a lengthy conversation about how I got into writing. As soon as I mentioned purpose and impact, it spoke to her and reminded her of the desires she had to fulfil. From that day, she asked my advice on which books to buy. I asked what kind of season she was in. She replied, 'healing'. I suggested starting with 'It's Time to Heal'. A few minutes later I spoke about the beauty of being broken, and in just a few seconds, she also bought Completion.

I did not have to change who I am to get the books sold or try to be someone I was not. Ladies and gentlemen, when I tell you how important it is to be YOU, it will make you consider your ways. What if I changed the website to a quote from my book and disregarded Jeremiah 29:11? This is one of my favourite scriptures that keeps me going. ***When people try to change you, do not let it happen***. If you don't have support around, do not let that cause you to lose sleep. It is not worth the nights of stress. Life won't always be fair, this I know, but when we come to a place of surrender, it really makes all the difference.

I nearly put my own needs first rather than God's needs and that in itself is a dangerous move. We make mistakes and are far from perfect, but it does not give us the right to live anyhow or do what we feel like doing because our emotions tell us to. At times emotions will take advantage and make you assume you are better than everyone else, but don't entertain them. Remain humble because people are watching.

You need to lay it all down before you can be free. I remember going to a dear friend, Ebony's book launch in December 2018. Guest speaker and author, Ruky Obahor demonstrated with Ebony the way in which we carry our burdens and try to handle life in our own way. Ebony carried heaps of bags and jackets, whilst her book (Beauty for Ashes) was in Ruky's hands. Ruky said, "Why not take this book?" Ebony replied, "I can't". She was carrying too many things in her hands that she couldn't see her way clear. We too can be like this where we choose to handle life in our own terms. The crowd was inspired by the demonstration and eventually, Ebony was able to put the bag and jacket down to accept the book. This is FREEDOM!

Picture yourself leaving all your problems, concerns, anxious thoughts to one side, and I don't just mean traveling for two weeks then coming back and picking up the pieces. I am emphasising on leaving your worries alone, for GOOD! Not worrying about what other people define you as or worrying about the status of where you are at this moment in time. It is about being secure in the season you are in and using it as an opportunity to get to the next level. When you reach that level, ensure your character will help you stay there. In as much as we must surrender, it is important to surrender with humility; not boasting about your successes but allowing them to build your character.

Character is always going to be tested in the good and the bad, but what makes an authentic successful character is staying positive regardless of the pain. Do you know how many times I've had my days of worry, only to discover there was no basis, as nothing happened? The fear of losing a job, the fear of not getting married before 30, the fear of not getting a business partner; listen, I have been there, and many more are going to go through this phase. But be encouraged - it is building your character and patience levels. Just because someone has obtained what you want does not mean that it will not happen. If God can do it for them, He will surely do it for you at His appointed time.

I'll leave you with this quote from a sermon by TD Jakes (2019), entitled, *Go after God's heart*:

"Reputation is what other people think of you; Character is what we are on the inside"

Surrender is a work in progress. It takes a lot of energy, investment and commitment in being free and allows you to make mistakes so you can learn from them. Do not underestimate who you are or what you have been called to do. Remember, working on your character has to come with giving up what you had in mind about yourself.

Even when it seems difficult, I choose to continue the journey of life, not worrying about tomorrow, but allowing my concerns and anxious thoughts to submit. It is important to have self-control in this area, not questioning why you are going through obstacles, but asking God what He wants you to learn from it. The more we can ask how beneficial our struggles are, the greater peace we will have when other turbulences come our way. It is a process, but with God on our side, all things are possible. It is He who uses our pain and turns it into a testimony.

I realise that on the journey to Glory, there are some responsibilities I can't afford to reassign. Instead, I choose to surrender my feelings and ways for His plans, not to allow anyone to get the best of my emotions to the extent of yielding. Do not allow anyone to make you deny what is in you. Surrendering is a daily process and it does not need the opinion of anyone else.

Towards the end of 2018, I remember hearing the words: 'surrender', 'letting go' and 'resting', as key resources to enter into the New Year. For those who know me very well, they know I work extremely well! I hardly take naps in the afternoons because my mind is focused on working, however, I realise that surrendering and resting are very important. I like to be a perfectionist, but I know that not everything will work out how I expect and that is okay.

One thing I do know is that what I may have in mind can't be compared with what God has in mind for me because His ways will always be better. (Isaiah 55:8). This is what gives me real rest; not worrying about how the outcome is going to look but allowing God to have His way. When I try to do things in my own strength, however, I do become tired, which is why I consider resting vital to the mind, body and soul.

From Glory to Glory

It is important to take time to rest, and at the same time work hard, so the keyword here is *balance.*

Stop Entertaining your Fears

I want you to get to the point where you trust what God says at the expense of His silence. What you ponder on, you magnify! To spend your life in fear, never exploring your dream is cruel. If you let fear take over your life, you'll never fully live. What is causing you to remain comfortable in the position you are in? Yes, fear will always be a part of our lives, but it does not have to live within you. The situation with fear is that it causes us to stay comfortable and somewhat stagnant. It is known for *(F)alse (E)vidence (A)ppearing (R)*eal. It causes deep depression to the mind and make us worry about situations that have not yet occurred.

We don't have enough raw and transparent speakers as we once did, who will take off the mask and show the scars and mistakes and just be real in front of the audience. *It could be that the fear of being judged is greater than being free.* It will take a while for one to open up with ease, but with time, it does become easier. It is the audience around that makes it easy to open up, however, we must understand that being transparent will help other people to open up also.

The only blockage is the fear of being judged and I fully understand. It is listening to someone else's story and telling them what to do, but when it is your story, you'd want someone to listen and not have control over how you should handle things. We should learn to listen with an open mind, and in love, accept and reject what is perceived to be good, as well as those words that don't fit with who you are. When you are the only one in your circle of influence who is excelling in health, wealth, social presence, accolades, rewards etc, the pressure to keep up with consistency can be overwhelming, which causes internal conflict. You can look at your own life and assume the person next to you is having it easy, but have you realised that people only show what they want you to see?

Those who are true will tell you how hard it was to wait for what they wanted. They will tell you how much they cried to get there. We are all made to relate to one another; we can learn to share our fears with people who are trustworthy and uplifting. Do not get me wrong, although there will be troubles, we can still choose to see it from a good place and grow from it.

I remember when I started my first full-time job in property. I did not have any experience or knowledge in that field, so I was basically a self-starter. It was difficult, constantly asking for help from the managers as I did not want to look silly. Eventually, I realised the mistakes I made were causing trouble for the company, so I was called into meetings to see what they could do to improve my working performance. I decided to use their constructive feedback to shape my knowledge to become a better consultant.

Rather than entertaining my fears, I chose to take them into consideration and have an open conversation with the manager to resolve it. Within two months, I was promoted to Senior Consultant, causing me to be in alignment with the nature of the role, including my confidence in speaking with clients and the sales/lettings managers on the phone. I learnt that it is better to receive feedback on performance than not getting anything at all.

Have you been in a situation where you told a few people about plans for the future, and all of a sudden they didn't come to fruition? Yes, I am sure we have all been there. The pressure you get from updating people about progress is dangerous, and eventually the pressure then turns to God, asking when He will answer your prayers. This is a word of advice: do not speak prematurely until you see results. Fear will make you speak quickly. I won't forget what happened in March 2016.

I remember securing a job for a Marketing CIPD company and was told it would be a three-month contract. Into the fifth day of the role, I was called into a room to be informed that the company did not need me anymore. I was deeply upset. On that same day, I went to my friend's house and literally, as I stood at her door, I started crying. I just did not understand why they did that to me.

I decided to use their rejection as a comeback to increase myself and my knowledge in writing which has now become a career and I use this to inspire other people to know that rejection will always work out for good. I chose not to entertain the fear of losing that job, because at the time, I was watching an interview with DeVon Franklin & Meagan Good sharing their testimony of their first book, and that reminded me that I had a book to finish at home.

When I say I hate fear, I really do! It is not a good feeling at all. Waking up worried, sleeping worried - when you feel an ache in your body you are worried. It's just all too much! What causes fear is the preconceived idea that something may or may not happen. Fear is one of the most powerful emotions we have and is linked to the way our minds and body operate. I believe the reason why some people can't get over certain fears is due to the fact that their issues have not been resolved internally, which sometimes manifests itself externally through abusive behaviour. In other words, they have not examined the 'root' of the matter. Instead, it is kept under a smile, pretending that everything is alright when in reality, fear causes confusion and stagnation.

Our preconceived ideas cause unnecessary thinking and dysfunction in our friendships and relationships. When you go through a painful situation, it is easy to take out anger and frustration but what will that ultimately lead to? Unresolved conflict. Fear only becomes big when we magnify it. This includes our thought pattern and what is currently going on in our lives - we use our current circumstance to define our destiny. May I remind you - never settle and overlook your destiny because of how life looks right now. Everyday won't be the same, and it takes great strength to keep enduring.

The fears we face are only temporary. Yes, there will be times of testing, worrying will be all around, but how you choose to react makes all the difference. Your reaction can either increase of decrease fear.

Too much entertainment and the opinions of others can also contribute to fear. We are too focused on what decisions people make on our behalf before we can make a decision. For example: "Ladies, what dress do you like – I can't seem to decide". The pressure to get everything perfect is like living in a dream-land. Perfectionism does not come from our power, because we don't have power the way God does.

In our imperfections, He makes us whole and complete. He reminds us that without Him we can do nothing. So why do we need to fear? I honestly believe fear is a waste of time and creates unnecessary stress for no reason. I remember a friend spoke powerful words to me and reminded me of an important but painful prayer. When you are going up in life, there are some who won't be able to come with you. It is important to remember this because as each day goes by, you realise that some people are in your life for a *reason*, a *season* or a *lifetime*. You just can't give everyone a front-row seat in your life. It's too costly.

<u>Why do we Worry?</u>

"Therefore, do not worry about tomorrow, for tomorrow will worry about itself. Each day has enough trouble of its own"

Matthew 6:34 (NIV)

Worry is useless – it won't change anything so why do it? Due to its nature, worry captures our thoughts and minds in seconds. Examine your life right now and look at the position you are in. I remember a time when worry would literally have me in bed with tears and I would wake up shaking. It caused me to check my heart because my thoughts were not healthy at all. I felt like my body was getting weaker due to the pressure I put my mind under. It felt uncontrollable. I had to take time away from social media, friends and work to recuperate. I know we all deal with situations differently but there comes a point where you only want your own company. I remember a friend said that when troubles overwhelm her, she would take a weekend off from work and stay in a hotel and spend time alone. It is important to take time out of our busy schedules to spend time with ourselves.

From Glory to Glory

Spending time alone gives you a chance to look deep into yourself and your mind, to monitor why you worry and what to do to prevent it from occurring. It is very possible to avoid worrying, although life has its challenges, it takes a lot of discipline to make this happen. When it comes to understanding the meaning behind worry, it will become easier to stay away from the burdens of the world. At times, when we worry, it can be a sign that something must change, rather than suppressing the situation. In essence, when God is calling you for greatness, it won't be the most convenient. It will cause some pain, but it will be *good pain*. We live in a world where we worry about our jobs, our finances, our friendships/relationships, our health, our children, our welfare, you name it. But what can worry do other than rob your peace and take time away from your day?

I studied Matthew 6 from verses 25-34 with two of my friends and we spoke from different perspectives on what worrying can do. It mentioned the birds that fly each day and stay in nests, yet we have comfortable beds and pillows, a roof over our head, good food to eat and drink. It made me realise how much I have to be thankful and not take anything for granted.

In my spare time, I was reflecting on the things taken for granted. It could be worrying about consistent income, or what to wear for a business interview, but before we get to these stages, have you checked the status of your health? Is your body in any pain before you pursue that dream?

You can, however, use worry to your advantage by always staying thankful. Do you know that being thankful causes you not to worry about your problems? It provides the opportunity for your problems to exit your mind and cause joy, happiness, and peace to enter. It's either we worry or choose to be angry and being angry with God is pointless because He is the only One who can help you. When you are thankful, you eliminate worry from your vocabulary and see the benefits of having a life full of peace and harmony.

I know the feeling of worrying, believe me, I do. I know how it feels when your body aches - you automatically assume you are ill and start running around like a lunatic. I know how it feels when you wanted to get that promotion at work, but another person was chosen for it. I know how it feels to worry about your future and what it could be like, but your goals and dreams don't match up with the finances in your bank account. Remember that no matter what you worry about, that is *time* wasted. Whether you have lost money or mishandled it, the good thing is that you can make money back, but when you lose *time,* it is expensive and can never be regained.

Choose not to worry about the things you can't control anymore. What is done is done and can't come back. You will never get back today, so when tomorrow comes, don't put your mind towards yesterday. *Focus on what is in front of you and work with what you have*. Worry is the thief of joy; comparison is even more intense but learn to discipline your mind. Each day as you wake up, picture worry as fire coming towards you. Who would put their hand in fire and leave it there for a few seconds? No-one! Fire is dangerous and if you are not careful, worrying can have this same impact whereby it slowly destroys the mind mentally, emotionally and even spiritually. Some people are lost in the fire and others are built from it. You choose.

I'm understanding though that everybody handles struggles differently, but it is up to you to allow it to shape or bring you closer to God. What we worry about won't matter in the years to come but will enable us to use what was in the past to shape us for the future. Worry equates to nothing happening. You're not moving forward and you're not moving backwards; you are stagnant. Training in mindful awareness is often a part of the treatment for excessive worry. Being mindful focuses our mental energy on the present with acceptance, which helps us relax no matter where we are in life.

Worry is by definition about the future, so training your focus on the *present* is a powerful way to reduce your worries. I met a lady at an event and could sense that she always had such a lot of thoughts, that I just could not put my thumb on what was troubling her. It would feel that the conversations were quite defensive, yet fearful. I could only listen and understand because when you have not been through what another person has, it can become very easy to assume.

Going through different upbringings has such an impact on how life is perceived. Some may have had an easy life, and others may have not had it as easy as it looks, but in the end, it remains a choice that must be taken into consideration. You either choose to be happy or unhappy. You either allow the situation to get the best of you or leave it out. Whether you meet people and they have exited your life, leave it alone. Whether someone betrayed your trust, let go. Stop allowing petty situations to get the better of you. It causes unnecessary stress. When was the last time you checked up on your health? Your own mental health? How about focusing on what is in front of you and not allowing people's thoughts or opinions to get in the way of decisions?

At times, it is the fear of how other people have made it in their lives that causes one to be full of apprehension. Perhaps you know of someone who is younger than you and doing great exploits, travelling the world, getting contract deals and paid speaking opportunities. You then look at your life and worry if anyone will notice you. I know how that feels. You then decide to look at your past and blame it for your perceived failures. We are all guilty of this but let's put a stop to it. It will not stop the other person or yourself from being successful, you have to keep persevering.

Don't bring someone else down to your level just because life isn't working in your favour. Learn from your environment and level up. Position yourself and speak success over your life. Moving from one Glory to another is not about looking back. Remember the word 'Glory' is powerful. Please hear me when I say this: do not allow the progress of others to deter you from your lane. Our path is not their path. You should know what your gifts are rather than trying to imitate someone else.

In today's society, we are so intensely obsessive about having control over every single aspect of our lives that it causes detriment to our personal health and well-being. Taking a step back and looking at what is making you worry can bring many positive benefits and will make you think twice before it leads to health consequences. Don't allow stress and worry to dictate your life any longer but learn to break out from it. Find something good about yourself and work on it.

I remember speaking at my friend's event in November and a gentleman came up to me and said I was a very natural speaker. I've heard this statement for quite some time, so I know this is where my gift dwells - in speaking. I wouldn't try to do something for which I am not trained or even had the experience, neither would I compare my public speaking with that of someone else. I can take a compliment, but to be compared to is a strong NO! Don't allow worry to doubt who you are.

"Am I really good enough?" "Will I actually get married?" "Am I going to be financially stable?" "How is it that I am not receiving enough followers on my YouTube channel when I produce good content?!" Do these questions ring bells? Whether previously or recently, please give yourself the tender loving care deserved and REST! If your life is about making everything perfect, I have got news for you - it won't. Please hear me, don't try to make everything perfect because when something falls out of place, it will be very difficult to get back up again. The amount of time you spend worrying can equate to the same amount of time used to invest in your life goals. Do not look down on yourself and speak negatively. Words link to worry and what is spoken will happen.

Even when something that is beyond your control does occur, how do you respond to it? Do you know that this could be a test without you realising? Perhaps that situation is preparing you for what is ahead. In order to get to the next level, we have to sort out our current situation. It is not wise to have so much worry in your mind while trying to fulfil that business goal. If your mind isn't in place, I strongly guarantee that the finances needed to support the business won't happen. Ouch! Yes, this is painful because it can be assumed the more money you have the happier you'll become. Finances are important. Yes, they are, however, if your mind is on other circumstances, how will you have intelligence to handle money?

Worry is a waste of time and energy if we know it can't actually produce any results. We may not know the full results of Brexit, but what we do know is by looking at what we already have. This is by being content and grateful for the things we possess and allowing what we already have to enable our progress. No matter what kind of news is given, we must learn to adapt and position our minds to learn something from it. Life can't always go the way we want it to be, but the best and most important lesson to discover is that worrying does not change the situation but causes a solution to be made. Are you the solution or just allowing the problem to become bigger than what it is?

Remember that it is hard to be genuinely productive and creative when we are worrying all the time. Its either you worry or not, choosing to take one and leaving the other. Moreover, I'll say this again; learn to **REST**. Your body is important too and needs time to unwind. Don't put yourself in too much pressure, where you are compromising on rest, in order to worry with the hope of making everything work according to your favour. This is God's role; let Him do a thorough work in you where you can just sit and relax. Above all, remain thankful because someone out there is wishing to have your life right now.

You Need Peace

Have you used prayer to calm down your anxiety and stress?

The same people who cause division are the same ones who have no peace in their hearts or lives. Lack of peace comes in various forms; division against friends, gossipers, uncontrolled tensions, fear of death, isolation, and criticism - you name it. My question to you is why we entertain these pitfalls in the first place. In particular, those who indulge in conflict will not get far in life as Luke 11:46 contributes, by warning us to be careful of these types of people.

Jesus said, in Luke 11:46:

"And you experts in the law, woe to you because you load people down with burdens they can hardly carry and you yourselves will not lift one finger to help them"

It's a very deep statement that causes heartache in the body of Christ and within our community. When you know something is not right, and choose to listen to it without taking action, you encourage the situation further. Rather than setting an example, your silence encourages the behaviour to continue.

Someone's *internal insecurity* can cause conflict. This could be evident in a group of friends finding the need to separate, for example. The person responsible for the conflict caused gets a false sense of elation, particularly as some of these friends would have achieved much, but this person's own plans has not come to fruition. Instead of trying to understand why life may not be going as planned, we find it easy to interrupt someone else's success which only reveals that person's heart in the end. It is frustrating to be in a situation where you can discern one's insecurity and then allowing that to be used against you.

When moving forward in life, mature discernment must be used to detect these types of behaviours and characters. This will be hard to understand but as you go up in life, be prepared to leave people in the past. Stop trying to make everyone understand your vision; they probably won't and may even draw you back. Don't force anything that isn't ready to be a part of your life. Seek God's peace and let that replace your fears. Learn to move on with and without people.

Before I go any further, I want to ask you this question: How are you feeling right now with your friendships and relationships? Score yourself out of 10 by trying the exercise below:

From Glory to Glory

(1 – 4) being unhealthy

(5 – 7) being neutral

(8 – 10) being very healthy

Please circle one number:

1   2   3   4   5   6   7   8   9   10

For those who chose numbers 1-4, write your answer below and discuss it with a trusted friend:

_____

_____

_____

_____

If you chose 5-7, what could you do to make it between 8-10?

_____

_____

_____

_____

If you chose 8-10, what advice can you give to someone who would like a healthy friendship/relationship? Discuss it with them and send a message.

_____

_____

_____

It is very crucial to be completely honest with yourself regarding these questions. No matter how much you want to hide your insecurities, our friends and loved ones should be able to give us peace of mind. For every relationship, there should be more positive contributions than negative energy and this is what causes healthy relationships to continue. Communication is the lifeblood of any friendship & relationship. The silent treatment and using an emoji to express how one feels only intensifies the matter. Having real peace comes through people you associate yourself with. I can look back over my life and count how many people have really contributed positively, negatively, or no impact at all, but it brought me to a place of strength.

Advancement often brings isolation and criticism, and God may be grooming you right now for a new level of blessing by exposing you to both! Can you handle it?

There may be people in your life who could be stopping you from progressing into the area you want to grow but holding onto them is causing delay. How difficult it is to let someone go, not realising that it will benefit you in the long-term? As long as it brings peace then it is very worth it Not everyone can be on the level that God will reveal, but are you still willing to aim for it, or remain complacent?

We should examine peace as a lifetime experience whilst we have time on earth. There is no need to pretend having peace with those around us if we are sincerely unhappy with ourselves. It is okay to be honest with people with mature and sound discernment; what determines strength is how you negotiate with people. Are you making compromises just to keep certain people on or buying your way through in their lives? If there are people who drown in their position of where they are, it could be due to their jealousy of how much you have achieved. Don't allow this to be your own barrier. Pray for them.

How many of us truly want peace? If you do, you have to learn to be a peacemaker. This is a vital tool to live a healthy, successful life. Peace starts within you and eventually blossoms outwardly, so there has to be a level of consistency when you are around others. We must learn to create peace so that our health, bodies, mind, soul and lifestyles are a reflection of it. The benefits of having peace are countless, but it is up to you to decide how much you want. Peace with family, friends and loved ones is a choice.

For me, when I am not feeling good about something I address it quickly because I know the impact it has on me. Peace comes from being transparent, honest and selfless. I remember a time where peace started developing in my life when I dismissed stress, and this was through having opportunities to speak with people who hurt me. I had to do it in love, not arrogance. You must be aware of what stress does - the unnecessary thoughts and anguish, for nothing. Your peace of mind has to be greater than the way you feel at this present moment in time.

We are all going through something, but until we can confront our issues and face our fears, how can peace be a part of us? Do you know that your peace is expensive and can't be exchanged for temporary satisfaction? When we wake up, our thoughts must be at peace, when we rest, our thoughts still have to be at peace. This takes daily practice. Take your body for example, when you rest, you don't feel it is out of place because you are still. This is how we should be when our circumstances become bigger than we can handle.

Over the past few years, I've truly been tested in the area of peace, and I've explained these in both my books, *It's Time to Heal* and *Completion*. It hasn't been easy; I can appear to look calm but deep down I have my days too. I cry just like you. I worry just like you. I fear just like you, but what keeps me going is purpose. It is purpose that grants me the peace I need to carry on. It's when people speak to me about how they feel and what their situation is, that increases my passion to help them. More importantly, I realise that it is not my peace, but the peace that comes from God. His peace makes our enemies be at rest with us (Proverbs 16:7). It takes great faith to get to this level, and it is still a journey I am on.

Remember that being at peace with yourself and others has to do a lot with the word *salt*. Why do I say this? In Mark 9:50 it emphasises that using salt is an expression of the taste and aura given towards other people by creating peace. Just as it is tasteless to not include salt in our food, salt brings the taste back to life. We all have a duty to ensure that our lifestyle, attitude and character carry invaluable salt that changes those around us, and as we continue to have this attitude, we will move from one greatness to another. This is what peace is all about. Do you want wisdom? Then have peace in your heart and learn to be complete in who you are.

"God gives wisdom to the wise and knowledge to the discerning. He reveals deep and hidden things and knows what lies in darkness, and light dwells within Him"

Daniel 2:21-22

Our Experiences Shape our Lives

What we encounter on a daily basis should not make us feel inferior or as some may put it, perplexed. Your experiences contribute to your own personal journey of life.

Our God has a perfect perspective on everything we experience, whether you are a believer or not. When I look back over my life, particularly when I was 21, I'd tell myself to open a business and personal savings account and invest money in both. I am understanding the importance of life, to be more responsible with what I have. Now, I can't talk for everyone, but as several challenges occur, it teaches valuable nuggets that we may not have experienced if life always worked in our favour.

It is when life gets tough, that strength is tested. Bitter days have value – they make us aware of our weaknesses and help us depend more on God. The times you cried at night, you can look back and say I was an emotional wreck, but through the lessons along the way, you grow up to love who you are and have emotional control over how you feel. What we all encounter may be regular, but there will always be a relationship between what you went through and how you feel about the situation. Starting with going to primary school, then secondary school, sixth form/college. You then have a *choice* to attend university to study your preferred course, work your way up in the corporate world, or set up your own business venture. All these ideas shape you because you made a decision. If I tell you that it wasn't on my agenda to become an Author, not a lot of people would believe.

From Glory to Glory

I'll share this with you - I got an E in Drama which I loved as a subject, however, I passed with a C in Business Studies which I disliked very much! I don't know why something I enjoyed did not favour me, but what I found difficult was favourable. Life will really present some funny moments, but you still have to keep it moving. Now I can see that it worked out for me because all that I do is focused on business now. Drama will still be a part of me, but not as much as business itself. Whatever you are good at, let that stay with you, and don't try to change. I can't say that I'll stop writing, because I started in 2012 with my journaling. It is a vital part of me.

Sometimes God's voice is clearest when we are in circumstances we don't prefer.

I will re-iterate, I did not like Business Studies at the time, but what I loved, I failed. However, in the process I learnt that God won't always speak on what we find comfortable, He will use those obstacles and failures to open our ears to hear His voice attentively. What we go through will either make us into better people or crush us back into our comfort zones. Be real and ask yourself what your situation taught you. To be real is the first step of allowing the journey of life to teach, humble, and position you into the person you've been called to be. You aren't living someone else's life, but your own. There is nothing that is in someone's life that isn't in yours. We can definitely be inspired by other people's circumstances, but you learn from your own and become better.

When it comes to misplacing something, it causes you to trace your mind back, right? I had this done to me so many times! I would put my comb on the bed, but 'mistakenly' put it on the table. As I am in a rush to head out, I mess up my whole room turning it upside down, looking underneath the bed, messing all the boxes and shoes, only to find out the comb was on the table. In this instance, I was forgetful because my frustration was more intense than my patience, to humbly take one step at a time to find the comb. I laughed because my mind said, 'I told you so!' It is vital to know where you keep valuables and take responsibility for it. No one else is responsible for your life apart from you. God's purpose is not for you to try and understand, but to trust that His purpose is good. It was good because I found my comb in the end!

Rather than me running around aimlessly, I should have taken the initiative to examine the room before making any decision. It is similar to when we are speaking with our friends, where there is a tendency to get our point across, but we don't train ourselves to listen. Instead, we assume that we know the answer. Rather than allowing this to become a habit, it should train you to take time to think before speaking. I will never forget this saying: *"**God gave us two ears and one mouth. Do the ratio!**"* We must discipline our minds to listen first, and then speak where necessary, not without wisdom or lack of self-control. In particular, with our words, they can create our destinies, so ensure that the words spoken are power-filled. God wants to help you grow by allowing you to see what only He can do when you admit that you can't.

You can also use what you go through to change lives without realising how many people are being inspired. I remember going to an event in December 2018, during which a lady came up to me after the session and said she'd been watching my videos on YouTube. This not only humbled me but encouraged me to do more. These timely words remind me that I have a continuous purpose to fulfil. Remember that when you know your purpose, you use it to improve your life, but you also use it to improve the lives of those surrounded by you.

When we go through uncertainty, it builds pressure. Pressure, if used wisely, can produce good results. These include a healthier mind-set to problems, being able to use what hurt you to make you a better individual, and more importantly, to help other people in their current circumstance. Why do our experiences shape the way we are? It is to prepare us for what is to come. Remember that perfect people do not stand on altars, which is why when facing pressure, it causes us to be vulnerable, but in a way that uplifts those around us. Our experiences are not meant to be a show, but a reflection of how God can use one's life experience to help someone who is near to giving up.

From Glory to Glory

Every drop of agony and heartache sinks down into the ground like a seed, waiting to sprout up into an oak of laughter.

I don't believe those who are in my life right now are an accident and those who have departed are in vain. There is a time and season for everything and our experiences will help us understand this. Not everything will stay the same, because if it did, we wouldn't grow. The more we grow, the more change occurs. The biggest lesson in your life is how you handle situations. As you wake up each day, it is a unique experience that yesterday can't take away.

Our fears and insecurities stem from guilt over past failings, but in the end turn around for our good. What we experience on a daily basis is shaping us to have greater days ahead. It may not feel great, but the outcome will be healthy and rewarding. We have no reason to be ashamed of what we have been through in the past or right now. We all have a story and depending on how ready one is able to share, it will eventually be for the Glory of God's Name. There is no shame in pain, just beauty for ashes.

The moth has to struggle in order to reach its full potential. If the moth escapes prematurely from the cocoon, it will be crippled for the rest of its life.

God uses our experiences to deepen our understanding of grace and puts within us a longing to help others in their struggles. When we experience unease, it isn't to be hidden and kept away but to use for uplifting purposes. There is someone out there who needs to hear your story, to be set free, and what is happening in our lives is a reflection of how we see God and can be used to inspire others to see Him. When I was in my season of job searching, people who thought I didn't struggle, were in similar situations, either not being able to pay bills or secure permanent employment. It is all part of the journey experience. Even our delays work for our utmost good. Delay does not equate to denial, and although fear can stem from this, we can learn to trust God's plan. See it from this perspective:

INSTANT GRATIFICTION = FEAR
DELAYED GRATIFICATION = FAITH

YOU CHOOSE!

2018 has taught me the importance of waiting, and may I say, waiting HURTS, but it is all a part of the process. My character was being developed. There were unhidden characteristics that could not take me to the next level, so they had to be diagnosed as soon as possible. I am not perfect, but what I desire is to be honest, selfless and real. I don't write to express perfectionism; I write to express brokenness, pain, and heartache because there is destiny attached to my name.

I am trying to analyse your heart to see how your thoughts operate. I want to understand what makes you cry, what causes you to feel anxious, what makes you doubt yourself. I use my life experiences to teach you how to grow and gain strength through the silent seasons, and how to understand your worth and value. Your story will save someone. Our generation needs a 'hearing-hand' - to listen. There are many unresolved issues behind the scenes and the only way to be free is through transparency. Be real with your life's experiences and in the end, you will come out as gold; gold that has been tested through the fire. When you can take time to understand your emotions and ways of thinking, that is when you are most effective.

I remember someone talking to me about family problems and it made me think twice about the things I encountered at the time. I had to humbly thank God for all that I'd been through because when looking at others, it is easy to think our problems are severe, not realising that others are finding it more difficult. Before you question life, listen to the person next to you and reflect on what they are going through. Our experiences have impact on the outcome of our lives; what we choose to dwell on shapes each day, and for this reason I discipline myself daily to never make assumptions without first talking them over with the Lord.

From Glory to Glory

I intentionally develop a thankful and grateful heart rather than worrying about how the day will look, taking it one step at a time and allowing life to do what it needs to do. I was pretty confident that I would do well, but I wasn't taking any chances. I was in continual communication with my Heavenly Father all the way, because life's experiences caused me to depend on Him always.

The Psalmist was a man with a wealth of life experience. The Psalms revealed moments where David felt lost spiritually and emotionally. Psalm 143 states that his heart was dismayed and troubled, in verse 11. In this instance, he paused and prayed that God would show him the way to go. He was able to trust God for his life. King David being a man after God's own heart, despite him feeling lost, was able to turn his direction back to the One who knew him best. In life, you will experience trials and tribulations.

"David's focus wasn't on his circumstances or what he expected God to do about them; it was on God Himself"

Priscilla Shirer (2007)

What kind of life experiences have made you hide from your purpose, due to circumstances? Yes, it may be embarrassing what you are facing right now, however, there is someone next to you who could be going through the same situation and needs a helping hand.

As I was going through my notes I composed these statements that uplift me in times of silence and I hope they encourage you too:

"If people don't use, misunderstand or abuse you, how would you learn to depend on God?"

"Why don't you allow other people to see your brokenness so that they can trust Me? You already know Me as the Healer but why not allow people to tap into Me?"

"I am already living in you but those around you are lost; they are struggling bitterly and when you have days of sorrow, you gladly approach the throne of Grace?"

"Are you complaining about the sorrow and anguish you are going through, not remembering that I put it there for my glory? For a purpose? What is the purpose you say? So that all men can be drawn to Me through your struggle, your tears and doubts"

The Lord's ways are mysterious and aren't always dependent on our abilities to even fathom or understand how He works. It is about using each life experience to sharpen our faith and develop our trust in the One who knows us better than ourselves. In His own time and season, He shall reveal the reason for our path in life, and Glory will certainly come out from this. There is no way God will leave you to go through pain without success attached to it. Your breakthrough knows your name and address, so be prepared when it comes knocking on your door!

--- CHAPTER 3 ---
The Solo Road

You can have a crowd around you and still feel lonely

The Cure to Loneliness

Please do not misunderstand this – there can be a lot of people in a room, but deep down, there are times when we don't feel understood. Completely. This is the truth. Everyone has moments where it feels no one fully gets us. When you wake up, who is there with you? YOU. When preparing for bed, who is there with you? YOU. You can be surrounded by everyone, but still feel lonely.

When I need to be alone I go to my car or find a room to meditate. Is there really a cure for loneliness? How do you define loneliness? Seeking validation from other people, getting 'likes' or comments will not cure your loneliness. At times, if we are not careful, we can use situations in our past that cause us to become stagnant and create loneliness in our minds. There may be a certain type of problem that emphasises feeling lonely, and then it repeats the process until it blocks your mind from thinking straight. Do not get me wrong - it is easier said than done, because when situations occur (as they will), it takes discipline to silence your thoughts, as the mind is the battlefield.

Our minds, like nature is like a vacuum that is full; it takes all thoughts and keeps it in

To live a stress-free life, it is vital to actively blot out unwanted memories and focus our minds on the present, not allowing the past to create a pool of loneliness. These memories should help to keep you going forward, seeing it as a tool to help other people who are lonely. There is a lot of emphasis on loneliness especially when seasonal holidays occur. A lot of people feel lonely when loved ones aren't around for Christmas, birthday celebrations, forgetting a wedding anniversary, but we must endeavour to keep going despite how we feel.

A lot of emphasis from social media is given especially towards teenagers and young adults, which causes them to question whether they are really up to the standard the world says they should be. I remember how much of a hype it was to reach a certain number of subscribers on YouTube and Instagram. (If you are not in the millions, then what are you doing?) So now one's esteem and validation are based on numbers? It is not always about quantity, but quality.

In other words, the content produced to film, is it helping others or just boosting your ego? Does your content appeal to the wider community? In today's society it is becoming more about what we can get out of opportunities and we must come to a place where we need to be honest and ask ourselves - what is the purpose that I've been called to fulfil? If this does not happen, our community will stay stagnant and nothing will change.

Do not be surprised about how the world is operating if there is nobody to stand in the gap. I know we may not always have the opportunity of helping the majority of people, but in your inner circle, who can you help? You do realise that when you are going from one level to the other, your mind-set and purpose will also shift. The higher you go in life, the greater the responsibility because people will be watching. This is not to be flaunted in such a way to suggest that one is better, but rather, by using what you know to help other people.

I attended a business event in December 2018 hosted by Multi Award-Winning Entrepreneur, Mavis Amankwah. She spoke on the importance of building a team. It's easy getting excited about building the vision, but you can't do it alone. There are several reasons why business and life can seem lonely; not asking questions can lead to a closed destiny. No matter how silly the question may sound, asking questions will give you answers that you were not aware of and can identify who you can partner with in the future.

In order to see yourself grow from one dimension to another, you need to firstly identify what is causing the barrier. I have learnt to reflect every evening; I do this during my journaling session to see what impact I have provided to those around me, how my day went and what could have been done better. I use honest judgement to see where I have gone wrong and sincerely express what I should not do for next time.

It is so important to have these self-reflective moments where we can identify what is causing loneliness to have access in our minds. I am still a work in progress; we all are. What I was able to understand from Michelle Obama's book, BECOMING, was through her experiences of growing up, she realised that the life she expected to have wasn't a quick process; it took heavy effort, tenacity and determination. Michelle is on a journey and so am I; a journey that is completely different to everyone else's.

Do have in mind that when you are moving from one dimension to another, it will not always feel comfortable, however, you can use this to your advantage and see that growth is happening in unknown places. Through your growth, you are able to inspire other people. One of the by-products of growth is that it alleviates loneliness, to identify strengths and weaknesses and helps to see what sort of insecurities are rooted deep within. Growth is uncomfortable, and so is being lonely, but instead of trying to bury it, choose to allow it to shape the way you think and implement it into a greater lifestyle.

Towards the end of his life, F.W Robertson (2010) made this statement:

"I am alone, lonelier than ever, sympathised with by none, because I sympathise too much with all, but the Almighty sympathises with me – I turn from everything to Christ"

As I read this, tears were streaming down my face because you never truly know who is there for you when you are gone. I cannot imagine the depth of pain this man went through as he wrote this, but what I can be assured of is that he knew Jesus was the real Comforter. The presence of the Lord caused him to realise that he was in good hands. The lonelier we feel, the closer Jesus comes to us. It is a responsibility for us to lay down our burdens so that we can be filled with His love.

The subject of loneliness cannot be properly discussed without exploring the uncomfortable thought that some people bring loneliness upon themselves (Selwyn Hughes, Everyday with Jesus – Wednesday 19th December 2018). When I read this, I was silent because we can play 'the innocent one' not realising that we also contribute to our own loneliness especially if we have not identified the root of the dysfunction. It is important to pause and consider that at some point, there may be self-generated loneliness causing people to stay away and avoid emotional trauma and stress - especially with anger and unforgiveness.

It is said that underlying attitudes can reinforce the slightest feelings of loneliness, and potentially drive others away. The only way to cure loneliness is to be a friend. Have you genuinely been a friend to someone else? By being a friend, you will find that other people are drawn to you, because being united with people is contagious.

In our challenging world we must realise that loneliness can become an increasing concern if nothing is solved. We must understand that the cure to loneliness is a mind-set shift. The question is, how can we really live in this world by ourselves? There was a time I came off social media for a week because I needed time. The minute I arrived back, I had lots of messages saying, 'Where were you?' 'I hope you are oaky?' etc. There will be times where being by yourself is important, but don't let it be for too long because there is only so much we can take by ourselves.

Could there really be a cure for loneliness, you might ask? I am confidently sure there is. Luke 6:12-13 and Matthew 3:13 record how Jesus had to take time to be away from His disciples and seek God to pray. This was not Him creating loneliness, but at times we realise when life becomes 'heavy', we need space. Anytime I feel pressure, I don't entertain it, but choose to stay silent and meditate, allowing thoughts of worship and prayer to sink in and take over. When I feel overwhelmed I gaze outside meditating on the wonderful works of God, how He made the stars in the sky, looking at the leaves as they fall from the trees, feeling the wind blowing on my face as I walk down the street. It is when one is still that one is able to really enjoy life, relax and take a breather.

I choose health over worry and won't compromise this for anything else. Loneliness can lead to depression and bitterness. Do not let this happen to you. Instead let your thoughts be pure, royal, trustworthy, kind, meek, and gentle. What you think on the inside will eventually appear outwardly through words and attitude. Remember, you can be distracted by your own insecurity which can cause you to create loneliness; don't allow it to, because your insecurities are not here to stay. They are only temporary. What makes you dysfunctional is not being able to solve the issue within, it is the underlying factor that loneliness causes when no-one knows your pain, your situation, or understands.

No matter who you are or the influence you have, you are still human and will feel misunderstood. Even famous people are overwhelmed because there is hardly any time for themselves. Getting pressure from every side is a burden causing suicidal thoughts. Our young generation face this pressure all the time. How many celebrities have passed away at such a young age? It was a shock to hear that Avicii who sang Wake Me Up, died at the age of 28, as well as Grime Artist and Rapper, Cadet. We may not know the full story, but they were too young to leave the earth. The impact they had on people in their little time here, and those left behind is painful, but it goes to show that no-one really knows what you go through, no matter whether you are famous or not.

It should not only be about position, fame, title or money that cures loneliness. Those that may not have as much as others, learn to use what they already have. What have you currently got that you aren't using, or are you abusing it? Are you manipulating people and causing loneliness to enter your heart? Remember that everyone you meet has a hidden battle that they are trying to cure. Learn to make someone's day by stressing less and reaching out to people more. You'll see the difference in your life because of the peace dwelling in your heart.

Stand out from the world's expectation and be different. Set a chain reaction of positive energy and see how inspired others will become just through your expression. It really is a contagious gift that not a lot of people have. When you meet people, how do they feel around you? Are they comfortable and can they have a decent conversation? Think about it, because it is deeper than you think. How you treat people is an indication of how you will be treated. Love on people and receive love back. You will see the difference!

Who Are You Really?

"For You formed my inward parts, You knitted me together in my mother's womb. I praise You for I am fearfully and wonderfully made"

Psalm 139:13-14 (ESV)

To deny reality is to diminish yourself and become less of a person, and the unreality will lessen your ability to stand up to difficulties in the future. How accomplished do you feel right now, out of 10 – 1 being the lowest, 5 being in the middle, and 10 being the highest. Be sincere with your answer. Do you believe you are fearfully and wonderfully made? A lot of people struggle with this as they only perceive beauty to be an external focus. How about your heart? As we grow in our walk with God, we realise that our outward appearance should not have any dominion over the way we feel; it should be focusing on developing our character and attitude towards ourselves and other people.

Refining one's character is a lot of work. I experienced seasons where my character was tested, especially when plans did not go the way I expected them to. There will always be a time in everyone's life where they will question themselves and ask who they are when their dreams seem impossible to achieve. I was reading about a lady who was born with Down Syndrome. When she was younger, she asked God why He made her that way and wanted to be like other people (Jenny Bryan 2006 and 2010). Do you get those days when you entertain comparison? You look at life and want to be someone else, but Psalm 139:13 emphasises that you are fearfully and wonderfully made, so why would you want to be an imitator of someone else when you were born to be original?

From Glory to Glory

It takes great faith to believe this. We are living in a microwaved generation where we want what looks good for a while but won't last in the long run. Most times, we are quick to believe in what someone says about us than to question if what one is saying is true. We freeze when someone speaks about us, making it hard to function. ***Please note: you have every right to discern and stay away from people who have no other motive than to bring you down.*** There should not be any element of fear in you when someone 'thinks' they know who you are. Really and truly, who knows you more than you do? Nobody! This should be a daily reminder for us; know yourself more than other people do.

A song I love from Hillsong is *Who You say I am*. My question to you is; who do you say you are? Yes, words can play a big part in our lives either to be dysfunctional or functional, but it is up to us to know who we are in Christ Jesus. It is not a time to be known for your branded clothes or the car you drive. These are important, but they are not your identity. When you question who you are, there will be certain people that start leaving. It's all part of the process. You can't afford to move from one position to miss the next one. How can you come so far in life to forfeit because of how someone defines you? It is costly to put yourself down for the benefit of others. Don't do it.

Knowing your worth comes in the secret place (Psalm 91). Your value isn't and shouldn't be based on what people think of you. Remember that you aren't called to please everyone. You are not anybody's god. There is only ONE GOD who we must please. ***Learn to REST!*** I'll be using the word **REST** a lot in this book, so get ready! When you rest, you are able to think better and have more time to improve your health, mental state and well-being. I didn't realise how freeing it was to lay down the weight that was on me due to pressure and fear. It was the intense memory of what people thought of me that caused me to shake off the feelings and be my authentic self. There are times where silence is powerful, especially towards the critics; however, there are other times where God grants wisdom to know how to fight our battles, starting with prayer.

As I was reading TD Jakes' book, *SOAR!* this statement spoke to me:

"I stressed that the problem was not the way others regarded them but the way they regard themselves"

Are you living in the past of what has been said about you? It is not what people say you are, but who you say you are. Each time you fail to realise who you are, there is a clue to your future success. It is teaching you not to depend on anyone for clarity or affirmation.

Don't let people be your competition, let them be your inspiration

Esther Jacob

I remember talking to my friend about the above statement and was reminded that people should inspire us to become better but should not imitate what they do. Do YOU! Who you are is not determined by what other people tell you to do. Are you different towards people and then normal when you are at home? It's frustrating being two people at once. Why change? Choose your battles wisely and maintain solid energy levels. Do not indulge in certain behavioural patterns that cause you to change for a temporary moment.

Whether you have the accolades or not, who are you? Whether the team is there or not, who are you? If you don't have all the resources and helping hands you need, who are you? I found it difficult to do certain tasks on my own in my early teens. I wasn't exposed to being independent until I completed my BBA degree and started having my own events and workshops.

True joy is an inside job that's not subject to people or situations. When you know who you are and what you carry, there are certain things that won't bother you like they used to. Joy starts with what is already in your hand, what is in your reach, how to use what you have and turn it around for your good. There is a lot of hype about the amount of money one makes; yes, it is an important component to life, but should not make you change. There are people who have survived with little or no money whilst looking after their kids and the daily battles of life. What makes these people stand out from the rest, is their hearts of gratitude and humility. They are exposed to what they already own and use it to benefit themselves on their level, not trying to be on someone else's level.

The more money I have, the better I'll be happy. Can you say this is true? What if you have the money and life is still the same? If you have a lot of money, use it to the advantage of supporting those who need financial assistance, or run online masterclasses and workshops; perhaps collaborate with other companies and businesses for the growth of the community. Don't use it to show off or feel superior to others because it is not a smart move. I would never encourage anyone to compare their financial status with anyone else just to prove who they are. If the money was taken away from you, would you still be true to who you are? You are not defined by how much is in my account.

Let this be a daily reminder - don't assume or write yourself off because other people are doing well with their finances and travelling around the world. You enjoy finances the most when you have hardly anything. Why do I say this? I'll tell you why: I've been to a few countries including Dubai, Berlin, Italy, Barcelona, Nigeria, Belgium, but out of these countries, do you know which has been my best trip? ITALY! Why? I'm glad you asked! I had no job at that time and didn't want to use 'lack of money' as an excuse not to travel. I tell you now, from experience, when you do not have a lot, you appreciate who you are and what you have left. Let this be a boost for you, to remind you that who you are isn't based on wealth, but on character, integrity, and humility. When all these fit in place, eventually the money will come to you; your passion must be so strong that people will want to invest in you just because of the way you carry yourself. Stop fighting so hard and work on your passion and build a wealth generation for others. Remember this: do not pray for money until you ask God to give you a good heart.

Moving forward, I used to worry about charging for events in the past because it has been said that the higher you charge for services, the less people would have interest. Is that so? Sometimes, we get to this stage and become indecisive which is very unhealthy. When you know your worth, you need to add TAX! Every investment, late nights and tears will be worth it; this is what makes you stand out from the rest and cause others to be attracted to you. Knowing who you are is also knowing what you will accept and what you won't. It is knowing when to speak out and when to observe and be silent. Being yourself starts with an inward character check which comes from a sincere place. You need to identify who you are from what you are not. This is not a time to look at others and say you want to be like them; yes, be inspired by others but do not allow that to block your own vision.

See the beauty in your flaws and mistakes and use them to grow and get better. Be better at all times and develop healthy barriers between your past and present. The future will come eventually, however, what you have in front of you is the present, so **BE** in the present moment and enjoy who you are. You are not called for everyone, so learn to rest and be still. Remember this as a learning curve as you wake up and go about daily duties. Know that not everyone is going to be for you, and that is fine. We only want progress and good thoughts. Nothing beneath that. Take time to invest in you and be focused on your goals. We all have a purpose to fulfil. Above all, God's desire is to have a relationship with you before anyone else comes in, so let this be a constant reminder.

Don't Create Isolation

"Be strong and courageous. Do not be afraid or terrified because of them, for the Lord your God goes with you; He will never leave you or forsake you"

Deuteronomy 31:6 (NIV)

Why are we isolated? Could it be because we try to do everything by ourselves, to the extent that we refuse to confide in anyone about our dreams? I know my parents give very wise advice on this topic because they know what life is. It is very costly to talk without wisdom, and sometimes words uttered can cause others to stay away if we speak too soon. Do you really want to be around someone who is always speaking defeat? This is what can create isolation. We do not want to hear one's complaints all the time; that is too much to handle. It is a habit that once it is built, becomes difficult to break. Remember that your habits will determine your future, so start examining your habits now.

Isolation causes barriers between our present and future destiny. There is always a gap between where you are now and where you are going. What are you going to do to fill in the gap in-between? There is a saying that if you want to go far, go alone; however, if you want to go further, go with two people or more. It is vital to know who you are surrounded by. Although people do not and should not define you, *don't create isolation because you never know who you need in life.* Don't be intimidated by people because they are doing well, it takes humility to ask what they did to achieve their goals. It is important that when you have people around you, you understand them on their terms. Sometimes you will be in situations when all you do is listen and be present in the moment; not to lecture, preach or tell them what to do. Do not be a dominant person but come down to their level and relate to their story.

Don't hide because people will see the real you; even if it causes you to be uncomfortable, just be authentically you. Remember that you do not have to be a perfectionist. According to Action Jackson, *"perfectionism is the curse of progress and completion".* No matter how perfect you want everything to be, it will never be. If you keep trying to make things perfect, you may chase people who are trying to 'be' on your level but can't achieve it. Do not make people trip up because of high expectations to have it all together. Be real and authentic if you want people to invest in you.

Our own doubts and fear can cause isolation because the energy (positive and negative) are conveyed to others around us. It may not show straight away but eventually, how you treat someone is the same way that others will treat you. *Do not procrastinate too much* that you choose not to make a decision. Be real with where you are and be sincere. No matter your position, God is still in control. You are not defined by the position you are in, but the way you see yourself. As mentioned before, perfection can cause frustration, which leads to questioning who you are. Remember *you attract what you are*; if you have a positive heart, you are more likely to attract the same people, and it works both ways.

When it seems everything is working against you, remember that you are not alone unless you isolate yourself. We are living in a world of brokenness. We use weaknesses to attack others to feel good; why is this the case? Is there an inner insecurity that you have not yet sorted out? All these questions are for you and me to think about. Meditate on them. Ask yourself and be real. *Can your own attitude cause your own isolation?*

I was reading the UCB *Word for You* (December 2018) about a New York businessman named Joseph Richardson who owned a narrow strip of land on Lexington Avenue. Another businessman, Hyman N Sarner, owned a normal sized plot adjacent to Mr Richardson's skinny one. He was offering to build several apartments that fronted the avenue, so offered Richardson $1,000.00 for the slender plot.

Mr Richardson was deeply offended by the low offer and demanded $5,000.00. Mr Sarner refused, and Mr Richardson called him a tightwad and slammed the door on him. Mr Sarner then assumed that the land would remain vacant, so he instructed the architect to design the apartment building with windows overlooking Mr Richardson's land. When Mr Richardson saw the finished building, he resolved to block the view; no one was going to enjoy a free view over his plot! 75 year old Mr Richardson decided to build an apartment building on it, five feet wide, one hundred and four feet long and four storeys high. Upon completion, he and his wife moved in. Mr Richardson and his wife spent the last fourteen years in the house alone. I want you to get this statement:

"Bitterness builds a lonely house with only enough space for <u>one</u> person"

From Glory to Glory

Do not make other people's lives miserable because things aren't falling in place. Our vengeance should not be towards others but instead, discipline our emotions and give all our worries to God. When you do this, you avoid people leaving, and in as much as there is confusion and unease about not trusting anyone, there will be seasons where God will bring people who we must learn to work with. Making your life perfect and seeing it from your own lens won't allow you to grow into the next level. Your life must start from one glory to another glory, but before you move to the next dimension, examine your heart and do a thorough run-through. If Mr Richardson was able to accept Mr Sarner's offer despite it being 'small' in his eyes, who knows how far they could have reached together? Partnership is everything. It does not help in creating isolation and seeing people move from your life.

According to the *Public Health Matters* blog, it mentions about social relationships being key to good health and reducing isolation. At times, we can create isolation for fear of what other people think of us, especially doing something radical such as leaving a full-time job with no alternate source of income or speaking to a large crowd of people for the first time. When we create isolation, it is to hide away from negative thoughts of others or to put on a façade 'living our best life'. No matter what life throws at you, it is not possible to be successful and alone. You need people, I need people; we all need each other. No matter what, don't create isolation but learn how to open up and ask for help. It doesn't cost a thing!

There are achievements I would not have attained if it had not been for the people around me. My YouTube channel would not have been possible if my friend Bukky didn't introduce her channel in 2014. Now I am collaborating with other people. You never know what is around the corner and putting yourself in a box is a big risk. Don't beat yourself up when things don't work in your favour but use it as an opportunity to get the right help. Even when you feel alone, don't ignore it. Be true to yourself and speak with someone you trust. I knew that I couldn't plan alone, so the importance of having the right people at the right time is vital.

It is an honour to have a friend who is wiser, experienced and willing to help you along the way. There is never a time I don't uproot negative thoughts or words that have been spoken. When words are spoken, it is easy to stay away from the environment, thereby making it difficult to communicate with others. Yes, I do believe that if someone isn't bringing out the best in you, it is important to lovingly extricate yourself from their presence.

When working and meeting people from different walks of life, it opens your mind to the bigger picture of what they had to go through. We are all relatable beings and can confide and relate with one another. There is no shame in being honest about a struggle and what one goes through. I remember telling a friend not to always stay in the house alone; go out and enjoy nature. Be around like-minded people. It is easier to stay home and watch movies but what is the ultimate motive? No-one can ever be alone in life unless they choose to be. My best advice? Speak out. Don't always keep your problems inside.

FAITH!

"Jesus replied, 'If you have faith as small as a mustard seed, you can say to this mulberry tree. Be uprooted and planted in the sea and it will obey you'"

Luke 17:6 (NIV)

God's Will for you requires being in the right place and at the right time; that is why He sets boundaries. Because someone succeeds in a particular area, doesn't mean you will and should feel inclined to follow their steps, however, learn from what they accomplished and work on your own strengths. Let God's timing be what you follow, not your own agenda. Your faith will be tested, and at times it will feel lonesome. But if you stick to the plan that God has for you, it will eventually be stronger.

From Glory to Glory

They say speak it until it comes into existence, right!? I strongly believe this. However, I'll be honest, because there have been times where I have walked by sight, and not by faith. I want to really challenge us to STEP OUT IN FAITH for what we want to see happen. Write down your goals, dreams, and aspirations to keep yourself accountable. There is no need to 'wait' until things get better. Start NOW because life isn't promised tomorrow.

I can't lie and say life has always been easy because it hasn't. To the man or woman reading this book, it takes utter STRENGTH to continually walk in faith! There are simply no words that can explain this. Faith is what will enable you to get to the next level, but you have to believe and have no doubts. You must get to a stage where you *doubt your doubts and believe your beliefs.* Don't wait for life to fall in place; position your mind first and let it take you where money must find you. *Those who know their worth will attract the right investment.* What makes the journey of life interesting is the faith we need to hold onto when we don't see our way clear.

I recall a time where my faith was being tested in worship. Rather than giving my all, I felt emotionally drained and unfocused. I chose to just trust God to know that He has my best interests at heart. I was looking round at other people and just by their facial expressions alone, I felt burdened. Eventually, I realised a heavy weight was lifted off me and my focus came back in alignment to God. I did not want to wait to observe people before I worshipped. I knew what worship meant to me so why did I have to wait? Faith is what brings you out of problems that you can't bring yourself out of. Faith can take you to places that your:

"Eyes have not seen, and your ears have not heard, neither has it even entered into the hearts of people, the things that God has in store for those that love Him"

1 Corinthians 2:9 (NIV, with emphasis)

On Monday 3rd October 2016, I officially started my first full-time job in real estate after waiting three years. Exactly two years later, I resigned from the position. I'll tell you why in Chapter 5. My last day of employment was Wednesday 31st October 2018 and was an emotional day. Two dear friends surprised me with leaving gifts, the management with leaving gifts, videos of colleagues wishing all the best for future endeavours on the TV screen, and so much banter in the office. I had a very good send-off (no-one had this send-off before!). It was a time of rejoicing, but also a time of real testing of my faith because I did not secure a job after leaving. My faith began the minute I handed in the letter of resignation. I did not know what to expect but I decided to take each day as it came.

If you want the prize, be willing to pay the price!

Faith comes with having full confidence in God and not having 1% of doubt. If you are intentional about what you want to see happen in your life, there must be intense faith. For those who know my journey about the job search, you'd realise that I battled with two requests: to get a good stable job and pass my driving test. At the time, my main focus was on securing a job, although I passed my driving test first. Either way, it still worked out well. For those who know how stressful the job search is, you'd know that it not only has an impact on the mind but also on one's health. Don't take it lightly.

Everyone reacts differently when it comes to over-thinking. Usually, when it comes to movements made, I prefer to be silent until deemed ready to speak, but when people ask, I like to share my story with those who want to learn and understand that their situation isn't for them but for a higher purpose. When you inspire to be better, it will take a lot of sacrifice and hard work. You have to be willing to be selfless because having faith is putting your ALL into something. It is about believing in what we have not seen happen and will fall in place at the right time.

Crying seasons will come, especially when situations have not worked as expected, and the reason many of us fail is because we trade what we want most for what we want now. As mentioned above, I had faith in believing for my driving license and job, however, I got both in different seasons. The driving license being in 2014 and the full-time job in 2016. It hasn't been easy, but who said faith is going to be easy? FAITH STRETCHES YOU! It is not meant to make you comfortable! When I tell you that 2018 has been a year of strength, it is literally all I've had to survive. I cry when I write because I know the amount of time and investment it takes to pour into people. It takes faith to still trust God when plans fall out of place. Remember, I mentioned that tears are a cry of surrender and a sign of great faith.

A time came where my mind was constantly occupied with settling down and buying my first house, but I had to be willing to walk away from the thoughts battling with my mind and trust God to determine my steps. I just stopped dwelling on my problems and decided to exchange them for His peace; to have faith in the One who knows my life. Even to the extent of reminding God about the promises spoken on my life, it was faith that kept me. I disciplined my mind and said that what I wasn't able to obtain now would be mine in the future, and I would appreciate it more by not rushing. As I keep growing in faith, I wait expectantly looking positively in the future than to rush and regret. This is what faith can do because faith isn't about looking at someone else's life for approval and validation of how yours should be.

The challenge for men and women between the ages of 20 to 30 are – what will my life look like in five years' time. You have been waiting to get married but what if the person you wanted to marry wasn't ready to commit? To the men, you want to buy a house before 30, but how are you managing your finances? Are your finances going on products that will eventually lose its value, perhaps fast cars? You may want to start the business, but perhaps your income is far too insufficient. It is okay to be honest about finances. If you do not have it all together, don't worry; there was a time I didn't have it all together myself, which made me start YouTube and writing. This was the time I used in my season of unemployment to invest in myself. The time you have right now, learn to maximise it because it is expensive to waste time. When you do this, you are able to generate healthy income, and not just one income, but multiple sources.

In TD Jakes book, SOAR! he spoke on the importance of speed and what causes one to be expectant. He mentioned that gradation is rooted in the word gradual which is where we pick up speed before advancing to another level. We will at some point be in this stage of transformation and change, and it's up to you to flow with the speed or forfeit the race. My faith is being tested every day and it's not always easy, but what is attached to it is peace of mind and good health. It's these nuggets that we take for granted. In moments of silence, faith is being tested, and when things don't 'look' right, there is beauty in this – you just have to ask God to reveal it.

There are situations that only faith can change. FAITH AND I ARE IN BUSINESS! You may say that your goals are high, but the finances don't match. Regardless of how it looks: FAITH AND I ARE IN BUSINESS! Yes, people want to see before they believe, but the God I serve wants us to believe BEFORE we see. There is a difference. Faith will make you feel uncomfortable, but when you want the blessing, how willing are you to invest in faith? There is no point in speaking without actively doing. Faith is a consistent routine for each day.

On Sunday 30th December 2018, Pastor Emmanuel De-Tumi ministered at my church and the theme title was: Greater Grace & Favour for Fresh Beginnings in 2019. He based his teachings on what we must leave behind and not bring into the New Year to start afresh. In Esther 2:1-9 focuses on Esther becoming queen, due to Queen Vashti not having respect for the King, as she did not want to go to the banquet. Esther had no parents, so she was an orphan. Thankfully, she had her cousin Mordecai, so she was able to stay with him. Eventually, she was favoured and chosen to be Queen for King Xerxes. It only takes a special grace and favour for God to bless you. He can do it instantly! God does not need your long list to bless you; it only takes faith as small as a mustard seed to see changes in your life. Esther was truly blessed and highly favoured!

Moving forward, what resonated with me was when the Pastor spoke about an appointment at the doctors. He cited a person who refused to take medication and as a result had become very unwell. He pointed to the fact that at times we can be quite stubborn and just use prayer and faith to believe that we will be healed without having to take any medication or tablets. In this case, the person had to revert to the medication. It can be foolishness/stupidity in the eyes of man to believe that prayer is the only way to be healed. If your doctor or nurse has given you the opportunity to take medication, why refuse? He added so much humour to it, but it is the truth.

On a personal note, I remember refusing to attend the hospital as I realised I had a little lump on the side of my breast in September 2017. It was a small cyst that was thankfully gone in seconds with a fine needle. This experience was harmless and did not hurt at all. When I tell you how much my head spun when I first found out, wow! I didn't tell anyone, not even my family. I did not want to acknowledge going to the GP, but I promised God that my faith was strong and decided to go. When I went they said it was nothing serious and that I needed to get a scan. It was one of my most challenging times, but it was faith AND action that got me there. As life is fleeting, I'm understanding the importance of investing in good health. Your body is precious so don't abuse it.

Each one of us has different symptoms in our body and we dare not ignore them. Do not use faith as a back-up and not take action! Sometimes God wants to see how much effort you put in something before He grants your heart's desire. If fear is higher than faith, then take a deep breath and try again. I will keep saying this throughout this book; health is wealth! Without good health, you aren't going anywhere. Don't leave it until the last minute; instead learn to feed your faith and starve your fears.

I am sure at some point we have been there because no matter who you are or what you have, life is full of ups and downs, and this is what makes life beautiful. As you reach new levels, faith has to be on the same level also. If you want to be a cash-buyer, you need wisdom to create multiple sources of income and cut out unnecessary spending. Your faith has to be strong enough to believe that borrowing isn't a part of your faith-plan but instead, working smart with savings and passive incomes. What reminds me of God's power and provision is Deuteronomy 6:10-11 (NIV) which states:

"When the Lord your God brings you into the land He swore to your fathers, to Abraham, Isaac and Jacob, to give you a land with large, flourishing cities you did not build (11) houses filled with all kinds of good things you did not provide, wells you did not dig, and vineyards and olive groves you did not plant"

This scripture will always remind me that what I think is impossible, only God will make it possible! When I have my moments of thinking whether I'll be able to achieve something in a short amount of time, I gaze at His wonders of the past and provision of the present. I have to look at my past to believe that my present and future are all part of His plan. I don't have to be afraid of what I don't yet have because the One who provides already sorted it. Your faith in God is what makes you achieve what your heart desires. Malachi 3:10 is another scripture I hold very dear to my heart. When you give 10% of your income to God, He *will open up the windows of Heaven, and pour out blessings that you won't have enough room to receive."*

--- CHAPTER 4 ---
Confusion vs Reality

We become more engrossed in the way society perceives life to be due to lack of identity and trying to fulfil it with the external

Social Media vs Reality

Social media is not my bible, nor is it what people have to say. I do not have to follow every trend that is streaming online to be 'up to date'. I do not need to define myself by the latest clothing, shoes, accolades or number of followers. Social media wants more attention and without it, there will be no rest. It's funny because I was speaking with my friend and we were talking about the impact social media has on our generation. Social media is you and me! You are not angry with the brand, you are angry with the 'people behind' the brand who upload constantly. Please understand me here. It is what we show on social media that can trigger us to feel bitter towards someone doing well, or have a sense of insecurity, or not feeling good enough.

In the same way, there tends to be criticism with several churches, we must come to a conclusion that church is you and me! It is not the physical building. *We take responsibility for what we advertise on social media*. The reality is that if you are living up to the expectation that you can't fulfil, you will drain yourself. Social media will control you if you give it power. Don't fall into the trap of becoming addicted to social media that you end up getting approval for every post. It really is not that deep. There are millions of people on Instagram and no one has time to be visiting every profile - that is far too much time.

It is easy to become glued to a range of social media platforms, from Instagram stories to Facebook live. The focus is on the next tweet a celeb is going to talk about. The focus is on trying to create a platform to increase numbers of followers without purpose or any good intention. What is the essence of having quantity but not quality to the lives of others? Growth without wisdom is dead. If you are too caught up in someone else's life you will always be where you are.

Remember that people only show what they want you to see; we all have secret struggles, envious thoughts and feelings that not even social media will understand. We advertise ourselves each day. We either get people to buy into us or move away from us. We can put as many pictures online to feel good, but when the number of 'likes' aren't what we had in mind, the self-doubt comes in. Why not be real? Let me put this in simpler forms:

Social media only shows the good sides of life because that is what it wants you to believe

Reality makes you realise how important it is to pray over your life and be real with how you feel

Social media has a lot of followers and fans

Reality shows that one has a lot of investment to do in cultivating real, raw, authentic friendships and relationships which take time

Social media always wants to be known for good accolades and no pain

Reality will make you see that not everyone will be for you and that is totally fine

Social media makes you live an *Insta-lie*

Reality will make you come to terms with yourself and be honest about where you are

Social media will put a lot of pressure to make you look like you are *living your best life*

Reality will make you see that your life won't always be in order or match up to what other people are doing

From Glory to Glory

Social media will work hard to cover up your flaws, insecurities, and mistakes

Reality will make you realise that no filter can hide your blemishes or regrets. *Just accept it*

Social media wants you to keep checking up on your adversaries and compete with them

Reality will make you run into the secret place and ask for a pure heart.

Can you see the pattern here? I have been guilty of this too. No matter your insecurity, you have to come to terms and be real with yourself before you can move on. Yes, it is uncomfortable to share personal struggles with the world, which is why we feel comfortable to show our best moments only. It is important to test your intentions behind what you share, whether you are doing it to show-off and make other people look small or doing it to uplift and remind others that they are not alone - only you know your thoughts and motives (don't deceive yourself). Don't allow someone's life to be cut short because of your extravagant living. There are people who have barely scratched the surface and managing with what they have.

In essence, social media is one of the greatest social interactive platforms to share ideas, stories, and can help start-up businesses and not-for-profit projects, but we should not make social media as a form of identity. I remember attending a Marketing Bootcamp in December 2018 and the teacher gave an example on YouTube; if it stopped running and no one could have access to their platforms, does this take away who they are? Or should it? You must understand that anything can happen. You can have YouTube or Instagram today, gone tomorrow. I still remember Hi5, MySpace and Bebo. Who else does? Where are they now? This is the reality of life.

Stop being frustrated on what you see; time does not wait for anything. The life you want to live is up to you; it is how you see circumstance that change the way of your thinking. Remember: *the number of followers doesn't indicate the amount of influence you have. Large followers do not necessarily mean you are making impact; learn to discern between purpose and promoting 'self'. Be wise.*

The real challenge is: are you really enjoying your life? Or is this a show behind the scenes that you want to hide? I will say this again: we only show people what we want them to see. Yes, you can feel a sense of accomplishment and approval when the 'likes' are flooding through your phone, even to the extent of pride. However, ask yourself if you are really happy in your season (with or without social media). Are you trying to create so much attention to purposely receive a false sense of pride on the internet? We all want to make it on social media, but be honest, not everyone is called to be on the internet. Not everyone may have the confidence to sit in front of a camera or speak to thousands of people on a platform - it is okay. Do not define your worth or identity based on number or activity.

Remember that social media is not running away from you; it will always be there. As Action Jackson would put it, *"post and go, don't post and scroll"*. This is targeted to the Instagram lovers. I have to discipline myself in this area because it is easy to keep scrolling and scrolling, by the time you know it, one hour has already gone and no work has been done.

Progress isn't about being forced down a specific path. It's about having more scope to live the life you want

My identity was never shaped by people's opinions because I am confident in who I am. If people can only see the real you on social media and not in reality, we must come to terms with that. What is the purpose of being popular on social media but not making any change to the society? My sister, Keeley and I were talking about the numerical impact society has triggered on young adults. There are a lot of people who have great followers, but the followers don't match the impact. Every day you are writing your legacy, so you are responsible for how you want to display your life, and I truly want to assure you that someone out there is looking up to you, so ensure that your words live up to your actions.

It can be a scary thing, though, having people watch your every move. Some may just be curious, but there are people who are really inspired by the way you talk, the activities and social networking events you have - you just never know. We must be aware that in as much as it is important to have a positive character and reputation, we do not neglect the importance of traditional friendships and relationships. What do I mean by this? I'll explain: technology has ruined the ability for many people to do simple things, such as meeting up face to face to have a genuine conversation. We would now prefer to use our phones to maintain contact, but it is not the same as having a real-deep conversation directly.

May I challenge you today, the next time you are eager to post on Facebook, Instagram, Twitter or YouTube, ask yourself genuinely, why you are posting – is it to get approval, or wanting to be known for the accolades? Or do you sincerely have a strong message that could help another person break out of their pain? Remember, if life is always about you, that is only how far you can go. Have a heart to help other people. When people see your posts, what do they see? Pride? Humility? The self-approval image? It is deeper than you think! People take their lives because of not looking a certain way or being up to date.

Social media can make people feel that they are 'left behind'. You are not behind on anything as long as you are breathing. I remember at college in 2009, there was a beautiful gorgeous medium tote tan Zara bag that was in FASHION!! When I say this bag was in vogue, it really was! I just had to buy it - why? Because I didn't want to feel left out. It's that sense of belonging that makes us feel worthy, whether that means neglecting what we currently have in order to obtain what looks good or currently on trend, but remember that fashion isn't always the same, and you'll be frustrated to keep up with it.

We can be tempted to build our social media platforms; yes, we are all building, but are we building with God? Remember Him in all things. I can't emphasise this enough, because without God, nothing will stand. Remember the story of the man who built his house on sand – how long will that house manage its position? (Matthew 7:26 NIV) When we are building our lives, whether it is a legacy, networking, or even in personal development, it takes a lot of discipline. You can also build a legacy on social media for good purposes. Billy Graham, for example, was a true man of Faith. Everything he preached was A class. He really lived till the age of 99. What are you using social media for? Don't allow it to pass you by without blessing someone else.

As long as there is honestly there will be peace. Our struggles not only help us grow in our personal walks with God, but they make us understand that life won't always be a bed of roses. We have to come to a stage where nothing takes our mind away from the purpose that is in front of us and still keep pursuing. Life should be enjoyed - yes, I fully agree. However, I believe that being honest about where you are is another step to freedom. If you do not like your situation, find different ways to change it. Starting with a heart of thanksgiving is one of the best antidotes to securing a peaceful mind and heart. It only takes one mind-set switch to turn off the noise and live a life on your level and appreciate your own lane.

Stop Creating a Fake Life

"You will be what you must be, or else you will be nothing"

Jose de San Martin (1960)

Stop trying to imitate or be like others; you are only going to drain yourself trying. It is a concern when we compare ourselves to others, to then feel insecure about who we are. We wake up in the morning hoping to see more 'likes', followers, business deals, contracts, opportunities etc. Perhaps you are used to receiving 500 likes on Instagram whilst other people have over 10,000. Are you really going to lose sleep over likes? Is that where your identity comes from? Just because people may not be supporting you now does not meant they won't in future.

I know at times those closest to you won't support, but that should not worry you. It is important not to depend on people for too much support to avoid disappointment. It is more important to have a group of people to agree with your vision and help it grow. I can strongly assure the ladies they are not missing out on anything! It is okay not to have it together, and I am not referring to being complacent or expecting less; there are times where you truly have to use what you've got to keep surviving. More of this and more of that won't necessarily equate to being happy.

A friend said to be a while back that "less is more" and it truly is! There is nothing in the world that will ever make you satisfied. You don't want to end up borrowing and being in debt for temporary attention. You want to create something real, long-lasting and eternal that will leave a strong legacy for other people.

People pay more for the unexpected, the scarce and the valuable. They will fall in love with the 'authentic'. Know your worth and add TAX!

You can't change a problem with external means; it starts from changing the way you think. When you live a life that is not your own, you drain yourself and have to keep up with it. There is no need to live a life that is not yours. The way I see it, if you can't afford it, do not put your eyes there. Learn to discipline the way you think and act because these turn into habits. Learn to accept your life for the way it is and if you do not like it, it is your responsibility to change.

We are naturally selfish. Point blank. We want the attention and desire of being loved. There will be days of tears to the extent of giving up, but it should never allow you to be complacent. Do not give up, no matter how hard it is! To even begin to remedy social media's problem with the lack of authenticity, we have to first resist the urge to believe that better more secure technology will fix the problem.

Now that technology is changing at a rapid pace, it triggers many teenagers and adults with information overload. Too much is being exposed! I've had friends who hardly use social media and text or use iMessage to communicate. I wouldn't feel any different if I took time off social media for a few months, and this is because I have disciple myself to have self-control. It is important to take time off social media from time to time and get your mind fixed on what really matters.

Your growth and elevation will require you to stop trying to meet everyone's expectations of you.

There is no social media platform that can fix your emotions apart from you. How can you move from Glory to Glory if you are creating a life that isn't yours? Be real with who you are, look at your situation and question what you can do to become better. Could it be to reduce the amount of time on social media and spend quality time with family members or visit your local care home and serve?

According to www.entreprenuer.com, it says that choosing 'friends' based on the assumption that they are like-minded is self-limiting, yet social platforms tend to make recommendations based on ones' set of interests and likes.

In other words, we accept what social media tells us to do and with what to associate ourselves with. This causes an indecisive person and potentially lost opportunities, because firstly, we shouldn't judge a book by its cover, and secondly, we must learn to give people the benefit of the doubt.

Be true to yourself and don't assume that because certain people don't look like the ideal role, they are not valuable. You'll be surprised! Have you heard of: *'fake it till you make it?'* Personally, I don't agree with this statement because faking it will only get you so far but being sincere with yourself will get you further. Your transparency is what opens doors for you because people want to be understood.

A tweet from a friend reads:

> **"Positive brokenness involves the intentional removal of inappropriate pride and self-reliance. When we experience the reality of brokenness we optimise healthy transformations which yield long-lasting virtues of truth and transcendence"**

We shouldn't wholly strive only to succeed financially and in wealth but to be integral. No matter what you try to cover up, the truth will eventually be revealed, so always be determined to live a life on your level. The lessons learnt from past failures are:

(1) I don't always have to succeed the way other people are succeeding

(2) I have to do the right thing under God's guidance and leave success or failure in His hands

With success, I am still a winner; without success, I am still a winner, no matter the circumstances because every good and bad situation will always work for our ultimate GOOD. There is no need to put pressure on making life the way you want it to be, just allow it to naturally be!

One of the greatest factor that has an impact on self-esteem is pride. The wrong type of pride can make you live an unauthentic life, causing people to only know parts of you, but not the real you. Always be true to yourself whether people support you or not. Those who know your value will invest in you. I'll say this again: **those who know your value <u>WILL</u> invest in you.** They will stand with you in the good and bad times. Find your confidants!

Whether you get to meet top bloggers/YouTubers including Patricia Bright, Jackie Aina, Shirley B Eniang, etc, they are doing what they do best because they have mastered it for years. So, do what you do best on your own terms!

"Your competition isn't other people but the time you kill, the knowledge you neglect to learn, the connections you fail to build and the health you sacrifice along the path"

James Altucher (2018)

Comparison does have a heavy impact on one's self-esteem. What thoughts are you feeding your mind with? Are you covering up the pain with lies for fear of people knowing the real truth? No matter who you are, there is no-one who hasn't and currently isn't going through something. We don't have to fake it till we make it. We must have FAITH in order to make it. If something is bothering you, speak out to someone. Be true to yourself; don't pretend. Find someone who understands how you feel and be honest. Comparing yourself to another will cause you to perpetuate being fake or unreal, buying into the pressure of pleasing everyone for nothing.

Author John Bunyan said if his life was fruitless it didn't matter who praised him, and if it was fruitful it didn't matter who criticised him

As long as your life is producing positive energy and effective results, that is what ultimately matters. If the work which you are investing in pays off, there should be no doubt or element of fear about what others say. Create the life you truly want to live by being your authentic self. If it is to serve other people, do it wholeheartedly. If you prefer being intimate, then build that strong connection. Don't try to be too much at once but focus on one step at a time.

Mr Bunyan was not focused on whether people acknowledged what he did, his main focus was to ensure that his life had meaning to others around him. Be free from creating a life that is difficult to manage and use what is already in your reach. Be you, above all, and learn to take time out for God to pour back into you. This is vital to living a fruitful and fulfilling life. Remember we are living for an Audience of One, not many.

Live Your Life

"For I know the thoughts and plans I have for you; these are plans to prosper you and not to harm; to give you a future and a hope"

Jeremiah 29:11 (NIV)

God's thoughts towards us are more numerous than the grains of sand! He knows our comings and goings, our beginning and our end. God is thinking about you all the time, even when it does not feel like it. I remember a dear friend said to me that when it seems nothing is happening, or life doesn't seem to go the way expected, it is when God is doing the most behind the scenes. My mind would go so far as to what I'd be doing in the next 2-3 years but was reminded to take life one day at a time (Matthew 6:34).

In order to live your life effectively, it is crucial to allow each day to flow naturally. If it is Monday, then let it be Monday, if it is Wednesday, then let it be Wednesday. It is not wise to say 'ah, I can't wait for this day to be over' and skip to the next day without appreciating the lesson of today.

When living our lives, we must also learn to mind our own affairs. 1 Thessalonians 4:11 (NIV) states that we should:

"make it our ambition to lead a quiet life and mind our own business and to work with

our hands"

You may want to question someone's motives as to how they made it successfully in their field. Word of advice: if you do not know what it took them to get to the position, do not interfere with their dealings. Your questions are not going to change them, neither their success. Do you on your level, and let others be themselves.

A friend came to me and asked if I'd like a car on finance. I told her that my first choice would be to buy the car as it will eventually depreciate with time. Whether you buy a car on finance or not, learn to be content. If you can afford it, go for it. If you can't please don't overanalyse it. We should remember what Apostle Paul said in Philippians 4:11 (NIV) which he emphasised; he has learnt to be content with whatever he has in all circumstances.

Reflect back to a time when you were young; you were eager to have the latest gadgets, but now life is teaching us to live within our means. We want to live the fast life but how will the end-result look like? The workshops Authentic Worth conducts is based on legacy. When you leave the earth, what will people remember you as? This question is serious; it is important to understand that each day as you live, you create legacy by your own character, attitude, and lifestyle; so, ask yourself how you want to be remembered.

Living your life means being remembered for good works, and as mentioned before, leaving a strong legacy for future generations. Work hard to earn the smile that no one can take from you. Live the life that only good people will speak of you and the impact you've made. The legacy you leave behind starts with how you live right now, how you make others feel, and in particular when promotion comes, how you handle people who are in a less senior position. True promotion comes from God and it is He who will continue to keep you stable. This is a big encouragement for me personally because when Jesus says yes, nobody can say no.

We must live our lives from a humble perspective. The life God promised us is beautiful, but it must also bear fruit. Every day is a gift so how many people are being inspired by your lifestyle? Can people see a change in you to inspire them to change, or are they just managing their lives on social media? What kind of reputation do you have outside that is different when you are at home? Let your actions be seasoned well so that other people will be inspired to live a good and fulfilling life.

Why do some find it hard to live a good life? I remember having a chat with my friend about the way we were brought up; some have struggled with severe difficulties and some haven't. In all honesty, there has to be truth in the way we live. Above all, there is no competition in the body of Christ, neither should there be between our family and friends.

Be Real

"And you, my Son Solomon, acknowledge the God of your father, and serve Him with wholehearted devotion and a willing mind, for the Lord searches every heart and understands every motive behind the thoughts. If you seek Him, He will be found by you, but if you forsake Him, He will reject you for ever"

1 Chronicles 28:9 (NIV)

It's really difficult to make much progress if we stay inside our comfort zone. Your authenticity will get you to a place of surrender. Being truthful is one of the ways God enters our hearts, even when we have closed it away from others. I am going in with deep reflection of being real with who you are. I can't emphasise this enough, because the person you may be trying to be isn't going to work. Do not *try* to be like someone else. When our minds wander, we tend to use willpower to steer ourselves back to speed. At times when we struggle, God wants us to be real, and to open up about our deepest concerns.

He is the ultimate controller of life, the inner peace that we need to keep going. When we go out, we don't know what may happen. Being honest about how you feel is the first stage of healing within. It is a vulnerable decision, but that vulnerability is what is going to save you and many people out there.

It is not only necessary to remove toxic people from our lives, but it is important to recognize when you are the toxic person as well. This may be hard to swallow, but at times we must be sincere with ourselves and see whether we are the cause of a problem. Are you having malicious thoughts about another person's success? Do we hide people for fear of them getting further? It takes a real heart to be this transparent. Let's take off the masks and be real, in love. If you are not building your friends up, then why are you in the friendship?

As we progress in life, situations happen - period. It will, however, take time to open up and be honest, and being real helps in a massive way. It allows you to sleep without fear, being able to build trust with others. There will be times when honestly speaking, it is hard. I remember being in my room and questioning why my prayer requests weren't being answered, and then I looked back on the promises and confirmations I received, to then understand why patience is a virtue. God's plan for my life does not involve looking back or any regrets. Let me be real with you ***IT IS PAINFUL TO WAIT!*** It is okay to feel uneasy for a little while to enjoy the blessings in the future than rush and regret in tears. If you sow in tears, you will reap in joy (Psalm 126:5-6).

When it is finally my time to be blessed, I am sure I will understand why the wait was necessary.

I may assume I know when the timing is right, but only God does. Yes, there will be people who say, 'be specific with God' or 'tell Him how you really feel' or 'do what you want to do', but these can be seen as fleshly desires, rather than allowing God to lead the way. I discipline myself in this area daily, to ensure that emotions do not overtake my prayer life, but also by being able to grasp the balance of being honest with God, yet humble and more importantly, thankful in all situations. The wait of the promise is painful but when the result happens, you won't be questioning why it took so long. You will be more thankful that the delay was not denial and the length of waiting caused you to REST.

From Glory to Glory

There is no need to covet what someone else has because no matter how much you want to be like the other person, God created us all with different gifts, talents, and aspirations. The stars and the sun are important for different reasons. We all have a special gif that can only be known if we take time to nurture it. Our gifts can be found when honesty starts. I know what I am good at and what needs improvement. I don't want to create a life that I can't live up to.

Being real causes one to stay alert of emotions and keep a high head regardless of what comes up. Learn to be powerful in your position and use personal development to keep you going from Glory to Glory. This is not a time to lose your mind or entertain any fears. You have to get back up again because there are people waiting to cheer you on, wanting you to help them.

There is no need to worry about how life looks now because each day gets better. When life seems heavy, I retrace my steps and see what caused it. I don't entertain fearful thoughts anymore because what is unsolved has power to control the mind. If there is anger in your heart, let it out. Remember that we are all carrying burdens so don't add more on to someone else. Seek peace and be in a place of harmony. A fulfilling life start with you. Invest in your life every day and don't take what you've learnt for granted. See the beauty in every situation and use it to make you a better person than you were yesterday. Above all, be real with who you are.

--- CHAPTER 5 ---
Life is full of surprises

"The Lord will surely come like a thief in the night, so at all times be prepared"

1 Thessalonians 5:2 (NIV)

Unexpected News

We don't want to hear bad news, right? We only want the good! But if only life was like this. March 2018, my eldest sister, Glory, felt pain in her tummy. My family decided to take her to our local GP. The doctor said her blood pressure was good, heart was beating consistently, and breathing was very good, so thankfully they were able to discharge her on the same day.

A few weeks later, it became quite severe. I remember Glory sitting on the chair after our prayer session at home and look very uncomfortable. The next day, my mother was about to wash her hair when she realised that my sister's stomach looked bigger than it did the week before. She was very concerned. So, my mum decided to arrange an appointment with the doctors, but Glory said she was fine and believed that it would go down.

The next week after that, Glory went to work and felt quite dizzy, and her amazing work colleagues, who I can't thank enough, took her to Lewisham Hospital on Friday 16th March. Towards the end of March, Glory was meant to be discharged, but the nurses kept telling us that she would have to stay longer. As a family, we did not know what caused her tummy to grow and the doctors could not seem to find the fault straight away. The hospital usually has their scans on a weekly basis, which we felt was quite long as it was a serious emergency.

We waited in the hospital for a month and three days, and that was when we realised that my sister was diagnosed with ovarian cancer. I can honestly say the hospital did not help in any way for leaving Glory in pain for such a length of time. Glory always had a big smile on her face, and I will always remember what she said to us, "If the doctors don't have anything nice to say, they should keep it to themselves".

We had countless visits from her work colleagues, church members, and friends who supported, prayed and encouraged us that everything would be alright. Glory would always say positive things and said she was getting better little by little. It gave me so much joy to see when she would stand up from her chair, dance in the bathroom and smile all the way through. She would use her toothbrush and toothpaste and brush without assistance.

She enjoyed our company and was always happy to see us when we visited her every day. We then spoke with the doctor who informed us of the news and said the only remedy would be to have an operation on her tummy to take out the tumour. My family was in shock and did not know what to say; we only wanted what was best for her life. When you are in a type of situation like this, the mind is all over the place.

Going forward, Glory was then transferred over to St Thomas' Hospital, Westminster, and was treated further. I was highly disappointed with the service from Lewisham hospital because they promised my sister would be out within five days and it took a month and three days! This is the reason why her tummy got bigger as the tumour was spreading. As a family, we chose to remain strong and trust God. As she was admitted to St Thomas' they spoke to my parents about undertaking Glory's operation. At the time, I was at work, so I couldn't take time off to see her, but thankfully my parents always communicated with me and my siblings. I will never forget Tuesday 10th April 2018 when the operation took place.

After she had the operation, my parents were desperately waiting for feedback to find out if it was a success. The surgeon mentioned it would take around four to five hours but took around eight. I remember calling my dad and the number was not ringing, but still, I chose to stay strong. I was at home then. A few hours later, I called my dad to find out whether the operation went well, and Glory woke up a few hours later.

I remember jumping up and down in the house with my siblings to tell them about the good news. I even recall when my mum was rolling on the floor just to wait for the doctor's feedback and eventually she too was happy.

The next day, the family decided to visit her after the operation. There I saw her, sleeping. Her face looked quite puffy, but she looked comfortable. I remember dad and mum being there on time, whilst my brother was at university and my sister was on her way from work. When Glory heard my voice, she was smiling, but could not move too much as a result of the operation. It felt as if she was still in pain but was trying to be strong for us.

My mum, my sister and I gave her a bath which we had to be very tender with, however, I noticed that towards the top of her stomach, the stitching wasn't secure and had to call a doctor to sort it out. Thankfully, they were able to rectify it. Glory just had liquids - no food at this time as it was far too early. She would always say she couldn't wait to get back home and dance in church. Glory was trying so much to move around and be active, but the pain was severe.

Following on, it was my father's birthday the week after, and I met two of my church members already at the hospital with Glory. After they left, we celebrated my father's birthday, which Glory was very happy about. She was told that the doctors would discharge her on Tuesday 17th April but would need to return the following week for a blood test. When she came back home following the blood test, she was really happy.

A week later, we had to go for yet another blood test, but then realised that Glory was not eating as much as before, so we decided to keep a close eye on her. My dad realised that her belly became bigger than it was even after the operation. I still recall Friday 27th April when we had to have her admitted to St Thomas' hospital again because we did not understand why her belly was growing.

From Glory to Glory

As my mum and dad arrived at the hospital, they had a meeting, during which we learnt that the tumour had come back. We were confused and wondered what had happened during the operation. It became so unreal from celebrating, to going back to the same process. The doctor mentioned that after the operation, the tumour spread to the kidneys, the lungs and different parts of the body which was quite difficult to trace. They could not do another operation, seeing that she recently had it three weeks ago.

We asked if there was any other treatment, but the doctor said that until Glory got better they wouldn't consider her for chemo. I had a flashback of a few people who had chemo and the responses were not so positive. It made me have concerns about my sister, especially for her hair because it was so long and thick! My family and I chose to stay positive. We had no other choice than to be positive and pray for God to intervene. A few days later, her stomach became hard and her feet stiff. We could not understand how the surgeon said he took the tumour out and came back so quickly, we just did not know.

Then I remembered how long Lewisham hospital took with my sister which caused so much delay and discharged her very late. When I say we were all positive, there was nothing else to it! My sister had more faith than us. She would watch TV, listen to music on her headphones and always give us kisses every time we had to leave to go home. She always made my parents happy, especially my mum! Wow, there was no time that my mum did not go to the hospital, to the extent that she slept there for a few days. My dad also was so encouraging and supportive, going every day to visit her. I love you both!

On Sunday 6th May, I went to Hyde Park with a few of my friends for a picnic after church. The weather that day was STUNNING! We had such a lovely time, whilst my family were in the hospital. A few other church members came too. As my friends were packing up to leave the picnic, I went to the hospital to visit my sister as I wanted to be with my family. I still remember the weather being quite bright outside, I saw her sitting in a wheelchair. Before, she was not sitting in the wheelchair, so I wondered what had happened. As I approached her, I noticed that she could not speak clearly as before. I asked my mum what happened to her voice and she mentioned that the doctor said the tumour has spread up to her lungs. When we asked if she would like food she would nod or shake her head. She would try to say something, but it was so unclear.

I had to call the doctor to ask if there was anything they could do to make her speak, but they couldn't. From that day onwards, it became intense. My dad was called just after 12.00am to get him to the hospital because Glory was crying and screaming. The doctor was considering taking her to Intensive Care Unit (ICU), but thank God, they realised her situation was not as severe. It was said that anyone who goes to ICU hardly ever improves sufficiently to leave. My Pastor, Rev. Dr. Steve Armah came to visit Glory to pray for her, alongside my parents, whilst my sister and I were fast asleep at home, so we were not aware of this until the next day. Thankfully, the next day was a Bank Holiday so my mum decided to stay with her for the night. I came with my dad to the hospital the next day and we saw Glory lying down on the bed.

As she began talking, we could hardly hear her. The doctors came in and had a word with my parents and asked them if they knew why they were called. My parents said no; the doctor said:

"Glory will not make it".

My dad replied, "What do you mean by that?"

"She can't live", he confirmed.

My dad said, "Well, if you say that, I understand; God is the Father and I am the care-taker".

It was such an emotional statement when my dad informed me and my sister of this. But nonetheless, let God's Will be done.

A day after that, one of the doctors said they had to stop taking care of Glory and checking her blood pressure. My mum was questioning why they would do that; she was not happy at all. She had a word with one of the nurses, and thankfully was able to get her checked. They said her blood pressure was fine. The nurse would give my sister tablets to ease/numb the pain, but she was not in a good position.

She would always make an attempt to brush her teeth, but she would never eat or drink. She wasn't able to eat for weeks. On Wednesday 9th May as I went to visit, I could see Glory was sleeping but as I got closer she woke up and waved. I too, waved back and asked if she was okay, she just nodded, as she could not speak. I then called my mum and dad to find out they were on their way. My sister also was on her way from work. Thankfully, about an hour later, my sister came in and she too looked after Glory. One of the nurses gave her a bath and we waited in her ward for her to finish.

Once Glory got back into her bed, she laid down for a while. My sister and I were trying to understand why her belly became harder and asked the nurse if there was anything they could do. Unfortunately, nothing could be done, we just had to remain positive. My sister and I decided to have a worship night. The song that really spoke to me at that time was '*Beautiful Name' by Hillsong*. I remember all of us holding hands singing it, and I felt in my Spirit that everything was going to be okay. I went to the toilet as I saw my sister crying, and as I stared in the mirror, I said to God, "In You I trust".

I returned and was still worshipping with her. She then went to sleep. A few hours after that, my parents finally arrived; a chaplain and a support worker came in the hospital ward to pray. We prayed like there was no tomorrow and we felt at peace. Glory indicated that she would like to go home on Friday, but my dad suggested that Saturday would be better. Glory replied, "two days left."

On Thursday around 8.00pm, I had to leave the hospital to get home for bible study with my friends. The whole family were there with a few other church members. I still remember when my dad told us that Glory stood up from the wheelchair and hugged him *twice*; it was as if she was saying her last goodbyes. "one day left" she mentioned. My mother being there to witness it.

Friday 11th May, in the morning, my sister and I were getting ready for work, when the phone rang. My dad picked up, but the person at the other end didn't seem to speak, so my dad hung up. The phone rang a second time and my sister picked up the call and heard my mum crying. It was then that she informed my sister Glory had passed away at 07.00am. What amazed me was that Glory repeatedly mentioned she would like to go home on Friday to watch TV in her room. We thought yes, indeed, she will come home on Friday, not knowing that God had His plans to take her to His Kingdom.

I do not know about you, but when you know it's your time to go, you really know. It crushed me. As for my sister, I had to keep her calm. My dad was getting ready to go to the hospital. My mother witnessed my sister passing away. I can't even imagine what it feels for a mother to see her own daughter pass away before her very eyes. That same day I heard the news, I decided to go to work, because staying at home was not the best option. I remember seeing my friend, Titi, and she knew something was up. She asked, and I couldn't say it fully, so I took it step by step.

Eventually, tears started to flow and told her what had happened. The way she cried with me was so strong that when I arrived at work it felt different. I informed the manager about what happened and was extremely supportive. On Friday evening, we had many visitors; family and friends rallied around us to support and mourn. It was one of the hardest situations of my life, especially due to my parents visiting the hospital every day. There was literally no day where my father and mother did not go. I salute them!

I had to make sure that my mother and sister in particular were calm. Eventually my brother, who was at university heard of it and broke down on the phone. It was hard for me to tell him as it was during his exam season. I thank God that he passed all his exams. What gave me joy was knowing that my sister knew the Lord and her faith was strong enough to indicate not only when she was leaving us, but she left at a specific time and day mentioned. She kept counting down the days, from two days, to one. 07.00am came and she lay still. The number seven means *completion*; it was God's Will completed in her life. We did not expect this to happen, but God truly did comfort us.

You may be thinking how can I still love and believe in a God who saw my sister pass away, yet continue to honour Him? As a family, we are rest assured that she is enjoying herself. Indeed, she has moved from Glory to Glory. Although absent in body, she is present in spirit.

Glory is my big example to persevere and keep going on the journey. Life is precious; cherish it before it is gone.

Just Accept It

"Do not let your hearts be troubled. Trust in God; trust also in Me (2) In my Father's house are many rooms; if it were not so, I would have not told you (3) And if I go and prepare a place for you, I will come back and take you to be with Me that you also may be where I am"

John 14:1-3 (NIV)

I had to accept it on Friday 11th May at 07:00am. I know that Christ is the main source of my acceptance and is the strength of my heart. Do you feel that when you have lost a loved one, you are tempted to question God? I have been there, especially with my big sister, but chose not to. I could have, but that would just have made the enemy happy. Why would I want to question a God who sent His Son to die for the world? Death is inevitable, and it is appointed for man to die at some point. We just do not know when, but we must be ready at all times.

I want to encourage anyone reading this book who has lost a loved one. Perhaps you still can't get over the fact that it is difficult to accept it. Know that God is the ultimate comforter and healer. It will take a long time to heal, I know. We all grieve in different ways, some quickly and some in lengthy stages; however, it should not make us stay down, but rise above.

There is nothing wrong with accepting that your loved one is not coming back. I remember having dreams of Glory with her bright beautiful smile, always buying the family so many goodies! There is never a day in my life where I do not feel Glory's presence, especially in her room. She has truly been a blessing to this family in so many ways, and what humbles me is her wonderful work colleagues who made her life super special. They treated her in ways unimaginable. I salute you, Jackie and Michelle.

When death happens, how do you handle it? This was the first family funeral I had to attend and did not know what to expect. Do I cry, do I break something, do I stand still? What would I do? All these questions suddenly surfaced. On Monday 4th June, I realised that I had to accept it; the flyer was done, and the arrangements were finalised with the funeral directors, and knew there was no turning back.

Regardless of how I felt, I sensed Glory transitioning to a higher Glory that could not be understood or fathomed. I had to be mature enough to take the tears, the thoughts that ran through my head, the silent nights that caused me not to sleep well at times, but through it all, I knew my family and I were being watched over constantly.

Meditating on 1 Thessalonians 4: 13-18 NIV, it reads:

"Brothers, we do not want you to be ignorant about those who fall asleep, or to grieve like the rest of men, who have no hope (14) We believe that Jesus died and rose again and so we believe that God will bring with Jesus those who have fallen asleep in him (15) According to the Lord's own word, we tell you that we who are still alive, who are left till the coming of the Lord will certainly not precede those who have fallen asleep (16) For the Lord Himself will come down from Heaven, with a loud command, with the voice of the archangel and with the trumpet call of God, and the dead in Christ will rise first (17) After that, we who are still alive and are left

From Glory to Glory

will be caught up together with them in the clouds to meet the Lord in the air. And so, we will be with the Lord for ever (18) Therefore encourage each other with these words"

If there is anything that has encouraged me, it is this scripture above. As I meditated on it, I was able to have inner peace to know that indeed, we will all depart from the earth one day, but it is unknown when. We do not know what age, time, day, we just don't. The belief that I have is knowing Christ Jesus as my personal Lord and Saviour, and that gives me joy to inspire other people who have been painfully scarred by the loss of a loved one. Accepting it is one of the hardest things one could ever do, always thinking about the good times spent and the long memories, but instead of me living in the past, I use my sister's departure to elevate and encourage others to share their story, because there is power in transparency.

Being able to accept this has caused me to examine my life internally and externally; what sort of impact am I giving to those around me, and how am I able to use my story to touch other people? It has made me more cautious and aware that each day is not promised, but because God dwells in our hearts, we can face another day. I know it is not easy, and sometimes when you want to be understood, it is easy to hear someone say: 'God is with you', but in that sensitive moment, you just refuse to be comforted, you want that loved one back - believe me I know.

Seeing my sister depart at 34 was far too young! But I had to come to the realisation that God's ways are not my ways and He knows best. I can't see the future, but He can. If I was able to control it I would have, but the power is not in me, it is in Him. We can try to take as many tablets, antibiotics, injections, flu jabs, you name it, but as we are living, we are also preparing for the other side. There's no cutting corners. In the meantime, I choose to accept it with the grace to carry on this race called life and continue living my best life possible. I won't allow this to hold me back and neither should you.

As mentioned in Chapter 3, I left my full-time job to pursue what I really wanted to do. Due to the drastic departure of my sister, her life didn't only bring Glory to God, but it inspired me deeply to help other people fulfil their dreams and not feel caged in a box. You don't have to wait until someone is gone before you start preparing. I understood that a salary can't and will never replace a person's life; it can't equate to the departure of a loved one. Money can be made at any time, but a life gone can't be retrieved.

I can now relate to other people who have lost a loved one, and decided there was no option to stay comfortable, but rather run with the vision to see greater results for the future and I am seeing it now. This is radical faith; I know it is not wise to leave a job without any financial stability but losing someone wakes you up and makes you understand that tomorrow is not promised, so do what you love now!

I was dwelling on how I'd make it, but then changed it around to how much impact I would be making to serve. My faith was stretched. The shock of my big sister leaving so soon gave me the determination to achieve much more. I remember telling my parents about resigning. I did not want them to worry, because I had planned to leave my job whilst my father was in Nigeria. It was only when he arrived safely in London I was able to inform my mother and father together. (If you live in a Nigerian household, you would know the thoughts that ran through my mind!).

I've never put myself to a test like this before. I am very strategic when it comes to my plans, but as it is, I knew my real intention for leaving was to inspire, transform and heal the hearts of the broken. You may still be in the indecisive stages of resigning from your job or working your way up for the promotion; either way, they are both going to involve hard work so keep at it and you will reap the rewards. It would be unjust of me to go through this painful road by myself when millions of people are still to recover from losses and disappointments. I am not sitting on my gift but using it as a platform to inspire.

From Glory to Glory

I had a book signing for my two books at WHSmith in January 2019 and was given the opportunity to speak at Barclays Bank for Women in Business and my previous University on Mental Health in March 2019. Had I been comfortable, I would have missed these profound opportunities. This was not me being hard on myself, it was a lesson that I'd learnt when death came knocking - to wake up and fulfil my purpose whilst I am breathing. You realise how important it is to not waste time on a decision and just do it.

My previous manager was very supportive of what I decided to do. This has indeed become a reality, which I must humbly thank God, my family, and friends for. The support is amazing! If this did not happen, I may not have known how strong my faith is. I did not know what to do because the way I grieved was in the mind, and it took me a while to grieve in tears. I could not cry when everyone else was crying. Even when we visited Glory at the cemetery, I just stared, and my mind was wandering.

My mind focused on my family, especially my mother who I wanted to be calm, and not worry. I had to realise that this was not a dream, but a reality. I would always say in my mind that if she'd open the front door one more time and say, "hello, hello hello!" it would wipe all our tears away, but I understood that it was not so. Acceptance brings healing which starts from within, and it is important to know when a loved one has triumphed from Glory to Glory, you have to accept the pain to heal. You may be asking God to fix the void in your heart, but you have to learn to acknowledge there is a problem. This problem could take years to figure out, but the fact that you've acknowledged it at the early stages makes all the difference. There is no need to question anything because what is done is done.

The best thing to do is reflect on the good times with your loved one. There is a book that my family received which provides advice on what to do after death. It advised us to talk about the person so that it will turn our mourning into joy and keep us in high hopes. I remember reading so many people's stories of how they dealt with their losses and it honestly did encourage me. It had never occurred to me that I would have this experience in 2018, and indeed, it was the reality. For me, the real peace that comes from these circumstances is knowing who God really is. He will reveal Himself if you allow Him. I used the people who had lost someone in their past to encourage me, to hold my hand and know that everything was going to be okay.

There are three universal concepts that we share, and they are:

1. LOVE

2. TIME

3. DEATH

Some people believe in God, but true impact comes from when you experience who God is. There is a difference. It is inevitable that we have an understanding that we are going to pass away at some point in our lives, but *what is crucial is the gap between birth and death*. How you choose to live your life will follow you for the rest of your days. Remember that **LOVE** is expensive, **TIME** is something that you can never get back if used unwisely, and **DEATH** is unavoidable. Do not take your life or those of others for granted. Love hard where possible and be aware of these concepts described above, because we won't always get the opportunity to control them. More importantly, what is life if you are holding back all the time? Let life continue.

Remember what I spoke about previously, in being yourself and not allowing anything to take your joy or peace. No matter what, when earth is no more, the money will still be here. We don't take it with us, we leave it behind. The real and authentic joy that comes with it is knowing that Heaven is only one stop away; and indeed, moving from one Glory to another dimension of Glory. *When you are buried you will bloom*. It takes strength because no-one sees when you are hidden, but in the end, you will come out as gold.

Now there is more emphasis on health than one can ever imagine. The internet and the news are full of healthy alternatives. It is becoming an increasing concern for many people to have thorough check-ups on their health and how they are doing. I remember after the news of my sister, a few weeks later I felt so bloated in my stomach and was getting concerned. Perhaps it was due to the fact that I didn't cry as much as my family did, because I still couldn't understand how it all happened.

At times the bloaty feeling would make my body put on weight and my clothes feel so tight. I decided to go to the hospital for a check-up and found nothing. It was just a lot of trapped air. My mind was going back to the way my sister held her tummy when she felt a sharp pain, so I did not want to risk it and just checked for myself. I was very hesitant to go and kept avoiding it, but I decided to get it over with. All this time, it was the battlefield of the mind causing worry for nothing.

"Is it too much to envision God bending over us on our final night on earth, tucking us in and kissing us goodnight?"

David H. Roper (2018)

Remember that according to 1 Thessalonians 4:14:

"God will bring with Jesus those who have fallen asleep in Him".

Imagine when you leave the earth, God pre-warns you in advance by ensuring that you are in safe hands. I still won't forget the way Glory hugged my father twice and assumed in his mind that it was a sign that she was going soon. This was something I had to accept, even if I did not want to believe it. Through it all, I have gained double strength that I thought would never come out from a situation like this.

Accepting this sort of news is hard to swallow, but eventually, as the days and months go by, it will start to heal from within and when it is accepted, gain strength. Of course, it takes time for each person to heal from loss, but it does get better. Sometimes, it is really nice to talk about the good days of the person's life; it helps to relieve the stress and sink into a heart of gratitude. My mum and I do this a lot and it helps especially the banter between all of us!

I would remember the times Glory would buy the family gifts including scarfs and bags. It made me smile so much! We should never feel our loved ones are too far from us; we should be encouraged that though they are absent in the body, they are present in spirit. Funnily enough, my sister's room still has the same scent. Nothing has changed! I know she is with us all, wherever I go, she is there with me. Don't let death sting you to be bitter; let it make you better.

From Life's First Cry to Final Breath

"From life's first cry to final breath, Jesus commands my Destiny. No power of hell, no scheme of man can ever pluck me from His Hand, till He returns or calls me home, here in the Power of Christ I stand"

In Christ Alone – Natalie Grant

Every breath we take is an opportunity to serve and glorify God. We laid Glory to rest on Monday 4th June, where family, friends, church members, and work colleagues came to pay their last respects. The church was full and people I hadn't seen in years had come to honour Glory. It felt so difficult, especially when I saw the coffin approaching the front door. I knew it was going to be very hard for the whole family, so I prayed that God would give me strength to stand strong. I refused to question whether God is real because no matter what happens in my life, nothing will stop me from believing in God.

I still know that He is loving and took Glory from this cruel world. I remember my beautiful sister, Nike Adewale who sang 'My Help' and 'You are my Strength' to encourage the church. It touched the depths of my soul. I didn't feel like it was real but had to face this reality. I must also honour my dear friends; Ebony, Jesse, Tracy, Maria and Ola who took time off work to support us at the funeral. Glory indeed was moved to a higher realm of Glory. She really did fight with all her might but what gave me joy as I mentioned earlier, was the fact she knew God for herself and did not give up.

In 2018, I have heard many stories about people who have experienced cancer, from both young to old ages; some have survived, and some haven't. But I have been encouraged at the same time that God has the ultimate say. I can't control anyone's life, and this was something I had to accept. The strength that my mother and father had in particular, to go through this was extremely breath- taking. My father is literally a reflection of me; strong and able to handle emotions. My mother, on the other hand, is soft-hearted, bold, but yet when situations like this happens, it isn't easy. If anyone knows how it feels to lose a loved one so suddenly, believe me, I do. At this time in my life, I have no other choice than to see God's hands in my family. Psalm 34:18 (ESV) says that

"The Lord is close to the broken-hearted and saves the crushed in Spirit"

Even when we are assured that our loved ones are in a better place, there is still this feeling of void because physically the person isn't there, but their spirit is.

The questions were unbearable when visitors came to our home because we could not understand why all this happened. I would be lying if I said it wasn't affecting me. It was an eye-opener, but I realised that through Glory's departure, there is something to be learnt. My life changed drastically; I was able to have more time for my family, to have workshops and events that will continue to inspire many more people.

Kristyn & Keith Getty's song, *In Christ Alone*, ministered to me at the time of my sister's departure:

In Christ alone, my hope is found;

He is my light, my strength, my song;

This cornerstone, this solid ground,

Firm through the fiercest drought and storm.

What heights of love, what depths of peace,

When fears are stilled, when strivings cease!

My comforter, my all in all –

Here in the love of Christ I stand.

In Christ alone, Who took on flesh,

Fullness of God in helpless babe!

This gift of love and righteousness,

Scorned by the ones He came to save.

Till on that cross as Jesus died,

The wrath of God was satisfied;

For every sin on Him was laid –

Here in the death of Christ I live.

There in the ground His body lay,

Light of the world by darkness slain;

Then bursting forth in glorious day,

Up from the grave He rose again!

And as He stands in victory,

Sin's curse has lost its grip on me;

For I am His and He is mine

Bought with the precious blood of Christ.

No guilt in life, no fear in death –

This is the power of Christ in me;

From life's first cry to final breath,

Jesus commands my destiny.

No power of hell, no scheme of man,

Can ever pluck me from His hand;

Till He returns or calls me home –

Here in the power of Christ I'll stand.

This song is so powerful; it reminds us that our lives are in God's hands. His eye is on the sparrow and watches each and every one of us. Even when it feels difficult, the pain we encounter now can't be compared to what is to come:

> *"I consider that our present sufferings are not worth comparing with the Glory that will be revealed in us"*

Romans 8:18 (NIV)

From Glory to Glory

Does this make you feel relaxed? Despite loss, there is still something that propels us to keep going. Every doubt is put on hold when I remember that God is the decision-maker. In Glory's departure, she has truly taught me how to live. To embrace life as it if was my last and to see beauty in all circumstances:

"Weeping may endure for the night, but joy comes in the morning"

Psalm 30:5

It Is Well

"When peace like a river attendeth my way, when sorrows like sea billows roll; whatever my lot, thou has taught me to say, it is well, it is well, with my soul"

Horatio G. Spafford

The reason I chose to use a quote from this hymn is because it was written by Author Horatio G.Spafford (1828-1888) (www.umcdiscipleship.org) who dealt with death in the family. He was still able to compose the comforting words of the song during the loss of his 2-year-old son in the Great Chicago Fire. I could not believe that despite what he went through, it caused him to say, 'whatever my loss, it is well'. This is really faith in action!

I also recall a time where two of my friends went to Liverpool Street. We met a man called Steve sitting at the corner of the Liverpool Street underground station. When we came closer, I could see that three tear drops were tattooed just under his eye. I asked him if he would like to explain what caused him to tattoo those tears. He mentioned that it was due to his child being burnt alive in a fire, and those tears represent *'eternal tears'*. This crushed my heart! Despite the loss of my sister which was just over a month, it made me realise that people grieve in different ways.

He was such a calm and humble soul, and he still believed in God despite what he had faced. I then asked him if there was anything he would like right now, what would it be. He mentioned 'a really nice home and bed so I can rest and put my books on a shelf'. He loved reading and that is all he wanted. I was greatly encouraged by Steve's testimony. God used his story to comfort me in my time of need, and I can confidently say it did.

Was I really saying to myself that it was well after the departure of my sister? It truly did not feel like it, but I had to walk in faith instead of fear. Who would ever know that a dear sister of mine would leave the earth so soon? This is where I felt my faith being tested. It's a time to reflect deep within and say with conviction that it is well with our souls. In moments like this, I sing out a love song to Jesus because regardless of what has happened, He understands how I feel. It may seem unusual for someone to say God is still good when their loved one is gone, and yes, there will be many questions asked, however, rather than me questioning, I had to encourage myself to say IT IS WELL and mean it.

Why is it well, you may ask? My sister was a lover of God and children. Her service in the church and commitment to the nursery were humbling. I would always see Glory assisting each child to their seats, distributing biscuits and drinks, and the children really enjoyed having Glory around. It has been a few months down the line and I've constantly had to say to myself that it is well. Even when it did not feel good, I refused to speak defeat. It takes so much strength being this positive. I've had a few people ask me how I do it and can only say, it's the Grace of God. When situations happen, you have to attract positivity.

No matter what, it still hurts, but what encourages me is knowing that Glory knew the time she was going. She knew her time was up, although we believed she would live very long. No matter what, we must say: it is well! We have to be okay with loss and grief; it is a part of life and of us. We will all go through it one day and others shall also grieve for us. Let us see beauty in one's departure, thanking God that He made a beautiful home for those who believe in Him.

--- CHAPTER 6 ---
Is your health in check?

How to Cope with Grief

"To provide for those who grieve in Zion – to bestow on them a crown of beauty instead of ashes, the oil of gladness instead of mourning, and a garment of praise instead of a spirit of despair. They will be called oaks of righteousness, a planting of the Lord for the display of His splendour"

Isaiah 61:3 (NIV)

My natural identity began in the womb, but my eternal identity began in the mind of God. The nature of human life is that each new generation begins where the last one leaves off. Who can offer advice on coping with grief? It is a blessing to be able to stand firm despite what has happened. We all cope with grief differently and there are practical ways of getting through a tough time of bereavement, some of these practical steps to consider if you are in the process of healing:

> ➤ **EXPRESS YOURSELF**: When people see me, they do not think I've been through loss because of my bubbly personality. I tend to hold it down very well, or when a conversation permits me to speak about it. I know the freedom that expressing yourself gives; it lifts up a burden that is laid heavily on the heart and causes one to feel free. There is no need to keep pain in because not only will it harm you but on how you treat others. I know this to be true, because when you don't release pain, you cause others to react in a certain way they may not understand. It is important to express how you feel the minute a memory or thought comes in your mind about a loved one. It is okay to be angry - don't let anyone stop you from expressing your emotions. Whether people may be thinking you are going over the top, only you know how it feels.

➢ **KEEP YOUR ROUTINE UP**: Among the things I do regularly at home including cardio sessions, I indulge in eating lots of fruit and peppermint tea; in particular I've enjoyed using mint leaves, lemon, lime, ice and water. These routines help me get in shape and keep my body in good health. If there is anything I've learnt about death, it is to not take health for granted. Consistency is a daily routine. When travelling on holiday, I read my Bible as it gives me encouragement and hope for the day ahead. It is vital to have a daily routine and stick with it despite the loss of a loved one. Yes, you may feel reluctant, but as you get back on track with it, you feel much better, with time.

➢ **SLEEP**: WOW! I love my beauty sleep! During the departure of my sister, there were times I found it hard to sleep; I'd assume she'd be knocking on the door saying hello, but this was not the case. Previously I mentioned that I hardly take naps during the day because my body isn't used to it, but once in a while it is good to take power-naps. Resting in the afternoon gives you strength to carry on the rest of the day and helps you function mentally. I usually have between 6-8 hours of rest each day. Take advantage and sleep (but not for too long!)

➢ **EAT HEALTHILY**: A well healthy balanced diet will help you cope. I realised that when I was bloated, I cut down on carbs and was cautious of food portions. It is important to know what you are putting in your body, and in particular, how well your digestive system is. I am very blessed to have a fast metabolism, so it wasn't an issue. However, I was cautious about processed foods for preservation and chemicals that can be harmful to the body. Don't fill your body with junk food for comfort. Instead, indulge in fresh fruits and vegetables as an alternative. You are what you eat, and although results don't show straight away, it may have an impact on your health in the future.

➢ **SPEAK TO A COUNSELLOR OR THERAPIST**: This is a good and safe way to vent and release stress. You have the opportunity of being heard without interruption and it makes one feel valued. It is good to speak and be real with the person. Don't feel that holding back will cause you to look weak; it takes strength to speak out. It is okay to have someone encourage and support you - remember you are not alone. Qualified counsellors and therapists give suitable advice in times of grief. We need to do the fundamental activities, including speaking out at the right time.

We all cope with grief differently. Some adults don't always want to cry in front of their children as it will make them cry. I really see crying in front of your loved ones as a sign of strength because it's real, honest and shows vulnerability. There is beauty in children seeing their mother or father cry. I remember times where my parents had cried in front of me, and yes it did hurt, but at the same time I saw strength. Even though we have parents who are meant to strengthen and build us up, there are times when they will need to cry.

I still remember when my father cried in the hospital ward for my sister because of the pain she was in. That shows deep love and concern. It is not easy seeing a loved one go through this, but it really did strengthen me. When coping with grief, if you need to shout, please do, if you need to break something, do it, but make sure you clean it up after! That aside, please be true to yourself. More importantly adults should ensure that their children are in good hands and not feel any less because of it. Be real with your feelings, it is okay to be angry, but don't allow this to live in you for the rest of your life.

It takes time for people to come around; others need to be away from the environment they are in. Some just need silence and time alone. 2 Corinthians 1:3-11 (NIV) teaches about the comfort that is given in our troubles:

"so that we can comfort those in any trouble with the comfort we receive from God"

It truly humbles me when I get people to speak about their issues; not only does it help me appreciate mine but makes me look at life from a different perspective. How could this be handled if it were me? I'd ask myself. I endeavour to give advice according to what I've experienced. Grief has been the most difficult and now I am understanding people handle situations in different ways.

Never forget in the light what you learnt in the darkness

When I experienced other friends going through grief, they were in temporary darkness and I was the light being able to understand and give them encouragement and hope. Now I am receiving the support which I am humbled by. When you are the light, you stand out from others and people are inclined to speak with you about their problems. This is a gift, so I am always intentional about how I utilise it. We must be able to carry one another's burdens and relate to them.

Do Your Research

At the time of my sister's departure, I was reluctant to do research on how cancer is formed and what caused it. I eventually started researching and realised that when cells in the body begin to grow and multiply quickly, it becomes uncontrollable causing the body over react. It is not enough to have faith and believe that everything will be fine. Yes, faith is important, but we also have a responsibility of individual research to take care of our bodies. "Prevention is better than cure". Our bodies naturally fight to prevent any sort of illness but as we grow, our bodies change. Take your time to invest in healthy food recipes.

I've always said this: I truly acknowledge, respect and honour doctors and nurses who look after patients and the intensity of treatments, advice, comfort and support given. When the nurse at St Thomas' hospital told me to do research I was not in the best moods, but I understood why.

From Glory to Glory

I wouldn't want anyone who has faced this to go through it alone. My health means much more to me than ever before. Even when the doctor requests to take certain medication, listen to the advice given. Do not try to be your own hero. Make sure you research thoroughly to get a basic understanding of what can cause an illness.

I was coming back from a training session when my right eye began to sting. I could hardly look at any screen, so did research on why eyes feel heavy and painful. I consulted my optician and thankfully they offered Systane Ultra Dry Eye Relief. The first time I used it, it felt absolutely amazing. It did its job! Even in times of fear and uncertainty, do your research. You don't have to spend so much time on it, but a few words and nuggets will help go a long way.

I know how tiring it is to research consistently and is not everything on the internet that is always true. Remember this. Advice on healthy websites that provide factual and accurate information on healthy maintenance are National Institutes of Health (www.nih.gov) and NHS Direct (www.nhsdirect.nhs.uk).

Be intentional with your health. Take time to invest in it. Health is one of your greatest assets.

There are many people who want good health services and the opportunity to move around freely. Don't wait until things get better, start now!

Your Health Matters

I have taken my health for granted; I guess I did not know what it meant to be healthy until death called.

Sometimes, what we are fearful of are the very same situations we must choose to go ahead with. I remember having a discussion with two dear ladies in September 2018 about mental health; the mind, body and soul.

116

How often do we go for medical check-ups unless we feel weak? That aside, I have been guilty of taking my health for granted.

Control the thoughts that run through your mind every second. When our minds feed on negative energy, our iron levels are low and eventually start to eat uncontrollably. Yes, food is lovely, but it shouldn't be our comfort.

Every part of your body as well as the mind is important, and here are a few key nuggets I'd like to suggest to practically take on board:

- Drink at least two litres of water a day ✓
- Try not to miss breakfast - eat a light breakfast if you can ✓
- Get a good night's rest - at least 6-8 hours a day ✓
- Maintain your personal hygiene ✓
- Keep active by walking, cardio, sporting activities and going to the gym ✓
- Check expiry dates and read labels on food packages including calories ✓
- Increase your vegetable intake ✓
- BE EMOTIONALLY HEALTHY & THINK POSITIVELY ✓
- **Take a break, travel and take time off social media** ✓
- Have your five-a-day ✓
- Make sure food intake is sufficient to strengthen the immune system ✓

The motto: *health is wealth* is something to consider seriously; without good health, you are not going anywhere. I now realise that it is not only what I eat that contributes to great health, but also my thought patterns and people I surround myself with. I take full advantage on health-care online and going to my GP regularly for check-ups.

Taking a break from everything is one of the ways to have a healthy, balanced diet. Having too much of everything is not good. Our bodies are made to function with ease. When we rest, our bodies are at ease and works better. There is no day that we should neglect how our bodies feel. Do not carry so much that your body can't co-operate. Do not overwork. We all have different positions and work must be done in order to survive but should not be to the detriment of your health. Take breaks.

--- CHAPTER 7 ---
The Importance of Mental Health

What is Controlling You?

"Do not be anxious about anything, but in every situation, by prayer and petition, with thanksgiving, present your requests to God (7) And the peace of God, which transcends all understanding will guard your hearts and your minds in Christ Jesus"

Philippians 4:6-7 (NIV)

No matter where you are in life, internal battles start coming to mind because we open our thoughts to fear. What you choose to focus on becomes your main focus. Know where to position your mind and keep aiming higher. Your eyes are tuned to what is seen and what is heard. What feeds you becomes your reality – when you wake up in the morning, what works are you declaring over yourself? Are you speaking positive words of affirmation over your life? The way you start the day will set a pattern for the rest of the day. Do not speak defeat over your life because the power of life and death is in the tongue (Proverbs 18:21).

In effect, balance is the key to living a healthy life both physically and mentally, as well as your work-life balance. If you allow work to control you too much, your body will be pressured to rest. It is important to take at least 1 day in the week to unwind and relax. It is a principle that has been shown to be physically and psychologically sound. God rested on the seventh day after creation (Genesis 2:2-4). The body of evidence and information is available on the Internet, concerning the importance of rest, recuperation, and work-life balance, and the consequences of not taking time to rest is almost overwhelming.

We live in a world containing the necessary benefits for our physical and mental well-being. The majority work tirelessly and often to the neglect of many priorities, but there needs to be balance. If we do not rest, we are in danger of wearing ourselves out. Many of us become anxious when we are separated from smartphones, iPhones/Androids because we are prone to know what the world is up to. Like many things, the Internet and all it allows us to access can become a distraction or a blessing. It depends on what we do with it, and how we use the Internet to help people in their time of need.

Being transparent and vulnerable especially towards young teenagers and adults will help them function effectively, being valued to society and their own circle of influence. No amount of judgment or condemnation will help, however, having a listening ear and being present are ways to get into their minds.

Proverbs 15:14 (NLT) reads:

"A wise person is hungry for knowledge, while the fool feeds on rubbish"

This is serious! How much wisdom do you want in your life? Does it only come through social media? Perhaps we check our social networks compulsively to see what is happening in other people's lives, but what is the motive behind this? You are what you watch and consume so be intentional about what you feed your mind on. Are we reading the right articles, getting the relevant information to encourage sensible living or are we being controlled by what we see? Remember that what you see isn't necessarily a reality. It is the mind that tends to pull us back into fear and complacency, especially when our plans don't always work out the way we thought it would.

Don't allow this to be you. Instead, break out from the routine of being influenced by the pressure social media presents. Instead, embrace who you are, your present journey, and where you are heading to.

Behind every success story is pain! With wisdom, we can make good choices and relevant connections that not only honour God, but also grants a life of true, honourable, pure, lovely and admirable blessings (Philippians 4:8).

Time is a gift that can't be put on hold. Time will not stop for anyone; we all have 24 hours in a day so there is no excuse to say there wasn't time to complete or to fulfil an assignment. Don't give your distraction power. Our minds need to be filled with pure thoughts and what we put our mind towards takes shape in the form of our attitudes and characters.

If you allow what others are doing to control your thoughts and purchasing patterns, it will cause you to be responsible for the outcome. Rather than allow the instant gratification to get into the way of your happiness and peace, why not take the opportunity to enhance a strong, intimate relationship with Jesus. Social media can be a massive distraction which is why I take healthy breaks from it from time to time. The minute I am off the platforms, I get so much done; I'm more in control of time and more importantly, my time with God becomes intensified. It isn't rushed or pushed to one side.

Distractions cause dysfunction and laziness. We tend to be controlled by business, politics, news, but despite all these, we are oblivious to what God has done for us, in His love. No matter your belief, we are human. God created feelings and we use them every day. However, don't allow the distractions of society to get the better of you. Mental health is a hot topic that strongly impacts our thoughts and lives. When we give in to things that are exposed to us and at times when we are most vulnerable, it is hard to make concrete and sound decisions.

According to the World Health Organisation (WHO), *"Mental health is a state of well-being in which an individual realizes his or her own abilities, can cope with the normal stresses of life, can work productively and is able to make a contribution to his or her community"*. (www.who.int – 30th March 2018).

Sunday 13th January 2019, I went to Belgium for a weekend get-a-way with a few friends. We stayed up very late that morning, around 3.00am talking about how pointless it is to take things too seriously. There is no need to worry about anything, because it is not going to change any circumstance, unless you use your circumstance to change others.

Mental health is a state of well-being and how the mind is able to cope with our day-to-day activities, despite not allowing it to have any dominion over us. The wisdom shared was not only thought-provoking but caused me to think about my purpose. We chatted for hours. Our vulnerability towards each other helped gain strength which in our respective seasons encouraged us to feel uplifted.

There is beauty in expressing how you feel verbally. It is okay to not have it together. There is nothing in life that should ever make you feel enslaved. Taking trips abroad is a beautiful way to relax, enjoy life and meet new people. We don't need to dwell on certain things so deeply. Let life be what it is and learn from what is already in front of you; avoid trying to make things work in your own power and take each day as it comes. Mental health is real and should not be taken for granted. There are people you may never know, who are going through severe mind-set issues that they can't speak about! Trust me, you would be shocked.

You have the ability to control whatever comes to mind, with the help of the Holy Spirit, as mentioned in chapter 1. Let go of bitterness and pasts hurts and learn from them in order to be free. Do not be your own victim to mental health, allowing it to control everything you do and say, and more importantly; remember not to make permanent decisions over temporary situations. Reject what hurts you and invest in what loves you.

Sometimes we fight in our hearts because we are not fully free. We think we are, mentally, but when a reminder pops up, the bitterness and tension take over. The book that has been a constant reminder to me about having a powerful and overcoming mind is **Why Forgive? by Johann Christoph Arnold**. If you don't have this book, I implore you to **buy it on Amazon!** It is filled with real and raw transparent moments and wisdom on the freedom of forgiveness, highlights of how people around the world found it very difficult to forgive because of how they were treated. It honestly broke me and made me realise that I have not been through as much as what others have faced.

It takes a heap of strength to forgive someone who is psychologically, verbally and emotionally abusive. Tension causes bitterness, which makes it difficult to move on in life. Forgiving someone may be seen as weak, but when you have forgiven someone who has done you wrong, it gives you power over the situation and freedom. There is true healing and freedom in forgiveness.

You don't have to live a life of tension with the past controlling you. The way I see it, I could choose to be angry and live a resentful life because of my late sister, but I chose not to. There are many people who have been through this and turning their pain into purpose. Up to now, I still get people asking how I cope – I reply to them and say, "Its God!" There is nothing I can do in my own power, even if I wanted to turn back the hands of time, I can't. What is done is done – what is taken away is taken away. The only solution I have is keeping it moving and not allowing the past to determine my future.

When sudden death calls, it causes one to mature and take life seriously. I have been called for projects and events that I did not think I'd been qualified for. Meeting God-sent people and having the right connections is only by His grace. I do not take them lightly at all; I choose to let go of situations and people who hold me back. This has been one of the most difficult situations I've had to pray about, regardless of the closeness of my friendships and those I'll have to leave behind. Because my life is in God's Hands, I trust Him to guide me all the way, regardless of who is around at the time. My eyes are open as ever to refuse anything that causes me to lower my standards. God has given us all free will to choose which way to go, and anything that does not serve, must go. I know what I am talking about. Not everyone can go where you are going.

From Glory to Glory

Whether you are allowing people to control every move and decisions, ask yourself why you allow the mind to control your happiness. The pleasure of approval and being accepted by others is far from who I am because I have been down that road before and will not return to it again. You like me, thank you; you don't like me, thank you. I will still be Esther because I know what my name stands for. Be true to yourself. Know what you will accept and what you will not.

Who are we working so hard for in order to be accepted? How can suicidal rates be high for fear of not being acknowledged? God is the One who desires all of us; He wants everything; our problems, frustrations, which is why surrendering is expensive. It is not only expensive, but uncomfortable, because you are not in control of your destiny. You have to make a decision to let go of certain things and keep pushing.

Persevering in uncomfortable seasons keep you going when nobody supports. Yes, the journey of life isn't an easy one, but it becomes better each day as it is exposing you to different lessons. You grow in pain, becoming better when it seems too much. However, only a few get the crown because they don't allow the external voices to define who they are. If you want the crown, keep pushing, don't allow the opinions to keep you stuck. Keep asking, keep searching, keep working hard, keep connecting with like-minded people. You will see development in your physical and mental health. Moreover, invest in a mentor or trusted counsellor. You don't have to run this race on your own.

You Create Your Own Fears

"So, do not fear, for I am with you; do not be dismayed, for I am your God. I will strengthen you and help you; I will uphold you with my righteous right hand"

Isaiah 41:10 (NIV)

Cutting people off can be very painful, but when you know where you are going, you will remember why a selected few can go ahead with you. Don't allow fear to blind what you know is best for your life. Love is the utmost but be confident in what connections to let go of and don't look back. Don't force anything to happen because everyone has a specific time, season and reason in your life. I attended Hayley Mulenda's masterclass in August 2018. She spoke about her journey and what it took to be where she is today. She inspires people to invest in themselves. She used her fears to create a pathway to selflessly *serve*. What are you doing with your life right now?

When last did you check your mental state? Fear starts from the mind but becomes to reality if you allow it. Do not allow the present circumstances to grip you with the unknown fears of tomorrow. Have you ever said to yourself, "I can't wait for Friday to come" because your day is not going as planned? You have to persevere! It is easy to think about the next day and not appreciate the present. I used to worry about my health, my finances, you name it, and I am not saying it doesn't try to come back to test my thoughts, however, I still rise because I choose to be a strong advocate for personal development. I don't want my readers to feel they have to handle their problems alone. The fears in our minds are based on how we choose to handle them.

Some people will be called for the platform stage; others will be called behind the scenes. No matter the position you are in, you are there for a reason. God will not grant what you can't handle. He will always grant what you are capable of achieving. Your strong points can be another person's weak points, which at times can make you feel isolated. Not because you are showing off or belittling anyone, but your gifting and skills are making room of progression. Whereas others are thinking 'what about me?'. It happens. This is why our world won't ever be grateful and will keep wanting more and more. If you do not learn to take care of what you have, it will be given to someone else. Stay in your lane mentally. Don't allow anyone to pull you back and more importantly, don't pull yourself back.

Wednesday 10th October 2018 was *World's Mental Health Day* and came across this message which reads:

From Glory to Glory

"Learning to gently reveal who we are is how we open ourselves up to love and intimacy in our relationships. Many of us have hidden under a protective shell, a case that prevents others from seeing or hurting us. We do not want to be that vulnerable. We do not want to expose our thoughts, feelings, fears, weaknesses, and sometimes our strengths to others.

We do not want others to see who we really are. We may be afraid they might judge us, go away or not like us. We may be uncertain that who we are is okay or exactly how we should reveal ourselves to others.

Being vulnerable can be frightening, especially if we have lived with people who abused, mistreated, manipulated, or did not appreciate us.

Little by little, we learnt to take the risk of revealing ourselves. We disclose the real person within to others. We pick safe people and we begin to disclose bits and pieces about ourselves. Sometimes out of fear, we may withhold thinking that it will help the relationship or will help others like us more. That is an illusion.

Withholding who we are does not help us, the other person or the relationship. Withholding is a behaviour that backfires. For true intimacy and closeness to exist, for us to love ourselves and be content in a relationship, we need to disclose who we are.

That does not mean we tell all to everyone at once. That can be a self-defeating behaviour too. We can learn to trust others, about who to tell, when to tell, where to tell and how much to tell.

To trust that people will love and like us if we are exactly who we are is frightening. But it is the only way we can achieve what we want in relationships. To let go of our need to control others – their

126

*opinions, their feelings about us, or the course of the relationship –
is the key.*

*Gently, like a flower, we can learn to open up. Like a flower, we will
do that when the sun shines and there is warmth.*

*Today, begin to take the risk of disclosing who you are to someone
with whom you feel safe. I will let go of some of my protective
devices and risk being vulnerable – even though I may have been
taught differently, even though I may have taught myself differently.
I will disclose who I am in a way that reflects self-responsibility,
self-love, directness, and honesty. God, help me to let go of my fears
about disclosing who I am to people. Help me to accept who I am,
and help me let go of my need to be who people want me to be"*

Anonymous

I can't agree with this enough – the person who wrote this statement
must know how it feels to experience mental health. Do not take mental
health lightly. We try to imitate others for fear of people having an
opinion. Hyping it over on social media and trying to fit in with the
crowd - I have been there and done that, and yet it is not fulfilling. As
you continue in personal life, you'll realise that you can't be everyone's
favourite. You have different hot beverages; peppermint tea, green tea,
organic tea, hot chocolate, mocha, coffee, latte – the decision is yours.
You can't drink all hot options in one cup! It is not wise, nor is it healthy
to try and be everything to everyone. Where is the self-control?

Have you gone to the extent of not knowing who you are in order to
please someone who does not know you? Mental health is what the
enemy uses to create division. For this reason, it is why people are quite
reluctant to open up and speak about what they go through, freely. Body
weight and hair loss are becoming great issues for many young women,
because of stress and over-eating.

From Glory to Glory

It is my deep and earnest prayer that you understand your purpose and fulfil it to the best of your ability before leaving the earth. Please do not assume that you are just a statistic. You are MORE THAN A NUMBER. It is statistically proven that half of all mental illness begins at the age of 14, according to the World Health Organisation, World Mental Health Day (2018) www.who.int.http://www.who.int/mental_health/world-mental-health-day/2018/en/

I remember speaking to my friend about the way our parents grew up, in comparison to young adults of our generation. I can't compare either, but there were a few similarities. Our parents may not fully understand the damaging effect of poor mental health on their children because during their days, the Internet was not as effective as it is now. We are becoming obsessed with what other people are doing, to the extent that we don't have time to care and focus on how far we have come, and what we can do to keep going. Instead, we struggle internally, break down mentally and attack physically.

There is a song that gets me thinking about mental health which is titled: *I need you to survive,* by Hezekiah Walker, and the words ALONE bring healing and restoration. When we think we can do life alone, that is total deception. At some point your loneliness will drive you to the wall and cry out for help. Do not take what you know for granted as it can help someone in their time of need, and don't allow what you know to create inner fear.

Allow fear to be exposed so you can perform to the best of your ability. Not everyone will get the vision but that is not the matter; the focus is to use tension to shape you into cultivating a strong character to inspire the other person next to you. Use it as an opportunity to keep going and growing. We need each other, no matter the situation.

SPEAK it to the Atmosphere

"Words can bring death of life. Talk too much and you will eat everything you say"

Proverbs 18:21 (CEV)

Wow! It brings me back to my knees, humbling and reflecting on words I've said whether in the past or at present or even spoken towards my future. We may think words are minor when uttered, not realising they are seeds that eventually grow with time. If you have said something unpleasant to someone, address the person with honour and respect and work it out before the end of the day. It is not healthy to sleep with anger in your heart. Our words have the power to enhance or break down. It is a daily decision to have self-control over what comes out of our mouths.

At a time I was feeling low, I was reminded of the power of words because how I handle my circumstances start with the mind. If you know about Romans 12:2 you'd be able to relate quickly. Your mind controls every decision made so, allow your mind to be free. Why is it easy to speak defeat over triumph at times? Have we not learnt to surrender as mentioned in chapter 2? As we let fear leave our mind, we are then able to move from one dimension to another.

When progression comes, certain conversations must be cut off. Don't indulge in unnecessary gossip or slander. There has to be a shift of you are to be impactful. If you are destined for greatness, be prepared for elevation that isn't going to be comfortable. Something has to change, and that includes the way you see yourself. Remember that words aren't seen but they can be felt emotionally and mentally, which is why it's important to speak at the appointed time.

I am aware that words can have an effect on different people in several ways, but how they choose to accept those words is up to them. When someone is provoked, I feel their energy, and rather than aggravating it further, I remain silent and allow the words to go in one ear and come out of the other. *If I can reject it in my head, I've already rejected it in life*. I don't want anyone believing that negative words have power over them. You have every right to remove powerless words from your life. According to Proverbs 23:7:

> *"As a man thinks in his heart, so is he"*

What you presume in your mind is what you'll believe about your life. What negative words have you been saying to yourself or allowing others to speak over you?

> *I shall have what I decree; yes, I believe it belongs to me. So, I'm going to speak it to the atmosphere.*

How intentional are you in sowing the right words into your life? There will be times when it will be difficult to believe something good, but we all have value, and that value comes from God. In order to see change, there must be a shift in your speech. I remember my friend saying that whenever she felt ill, she wouldn't agree. Instead, she'd say she was healed, despite the pain, because she is aware that words are powerful.

Our words are working towards our success and future – when you speak something into existence, you are giving it permission to manifest. This is why it is important not to speak out of emotions or anger because words are like a broken egg; once cracked, it's cracked. You break a glass cup, no matter how you try to fix it, you may end up hurting yourself even more.

I know what it means to be disciplined and careful with words and what to say at the appointed time. I've learnt in my twenties to understand that not everything has to be said at once, but instead, waiting to be in the right environment that permits me to speak. Even when a situation may look impossible, I don't add more doubt to it; I silence it with prayer and faith! What sort of change are you looking to see through your words?

The Importance of Prayer

"But when you pray, go into your room, close the door and pray to your Father, who is unseen. Then your Father who sees what is done in secret will reward you"

Matthew 6:6 (NIV)

I strived to unravel what I thought was a mystery, as I longed to learn the right way to pray. Eventually, I learnt that our prayers are simple and not complicated. I remember a time when someone said that they had prayed for more than 3 hours+. The Lord knows my heart that I've not had this opportunity to pray for three hours straight, but just by the depth and heaviness of my heart, He is still able to understand my prayer and still answers me till today! Even when I cry, I know God hears me, that is how intentional He is when it comes to hearing us when we pray.

Pray, then ACT! We are limited, but God is limitless. What you see as difficult, God sees as very possible. Learn to change and position your thinking and prayer pattern. Private devotions involve the discipline of reading the Bible, praying and spending time with God. This discipline not only draws us closer to God but also empowers us for public ministry. We must endeavour to pray for our breakthroughs to come to fruition. Through this, it opens doors of blessings; there is no prayer I've prayed that hasn't come to pass.

The most important prayer point is life. Having life is the first and greatest gift of all. Rather than praying for financial abundance, ask God to sustain you in good health. Trying to find a way to set up the business? Why not ask God for wisdom to help you build with what you have?

From Glory to Glory

The more prayer is practised, the stronger you become; it is in the secret place that prayer is used as a weapon. What used to bother and make you lose sleep won't be a problem anymore. Prayer takes away the stresses and anxiety of the mind and causes one to stand before great men. There is beauty in exercising and adapting to a strong and consistent prayer life.

God invites us to an intimate exchange through which He promises to listen through our silence, our tears, and groaning. There are so many different ways in which people pray, but what matters is the intention and consistency behind it. God assures that prayer is a real gift and an opportunity to honour His majesty and power, to display our confidence in His provision and affirm our security in Him when we feel unsafe *(as well as the prayers that run down our cheeks as silent tears)*. When placing our trust in something, we need to understand what is given back in return.

When you buy an item, for example, a dress, or a pair of trainers, you observe it, ask questions and see whether it will suit you. You try it on to see how it looks and eventually exchange money for the product. This is the same with God. We use prayer as a way of seeing how God will come through for us, praying with a humble heart that is surrendered and dependent on Him because He hears every prayer.

In times of desperate need, such as when I had to get a scan on my stomach, my first thought was prayer. Rather than me worrying, I decided to seek God because I didn't want to get a headache by worrying for nothing. This is what I needed, especially as I observed my sister being a pure example of praying for herself when she was ill. She didn't want the illness to be a barrier to her prayers. I am always reminded that in effect when prayer goes up, the Glory of God comes down. Prayer is a way to communicate with the Father for Him to work in our lives in the natural realm. When we ask God for financial provision, He grants the wisdom to create wealth, including our gifts that create paid opportunities. This could be public speaking or travelling abroad for a conference (all paid for) just because GOD CAN!!

Let us not doubt the prayers we utter because they may not 'feel' strong enough. Even as it becomes a struggle to pray, keep walking with Him because that is when our faith becomes stronger as opposition becomes intense. You will know when you are near to your breakthrough when prayer becomes difficult, but still, choose to persevere! Deciding to remain strong at the broken places is timely and becomes easier as we deepen our prayer life, not just when plans are going well, but should be able to pray regardless of what comes our way. I remember reading a statement from Carruthers (2007), which said:

"In the whole book of Esther, the word 'GOD' is not once mentioned. Yet, it is clear that God was at work. Our Father often works in secret, in the background. Be assured that right now, God is working and arranging things so that He can fulfil His purpose for you"

As I read this, my eyes were tearful. Just because I am a Christian, doesn't mean I don't have my days of crying – after all, to cry is human. I won't stay down, no I won't, but I like to keep it real and be true in how I feel. Prayer takes A LOT OF STRENGTH! Not just physical strength but also mentally and spiritually. It's like when your muscles are working – as your body tenses, your muscles build up, making them stronger. We can't see our muscles, but we know that they are working for our good. This is the same with God. When there seems to be silence or nothing happening, that is when He is up to His best.

I choose not to give up but to reflect on all the good things that happened in my life because if not for God, I don't know how my life would look like right now. The importance of prayer is to keep you grounded and humble in God; not to run your own life, and more crucially, to keep the enemy far away from your mind. The less you pray, the weaker you become. The more you pray, the stronger you become. Let this be a simple message to remember. Every day God gives you breath is an opportunity to pray.

From Glory to Glory

Understand this: *minutes* invested in prayer will give you a greater return than *hours* spent in ceaseless activity.

Yes, you will be tested in your prayer life when storms come. People may take advantage because you are still 'waiting for the blessing to come to pass'. There are so many ways God puts us to the test, but how badly do you want it? How much effort are you putting into your words and more importantly, what kind of words are you speaking over your life?

Your words are vitally powerful in good and bad seasons and what you say will lead to consequences. I've seen how much I've matured by being silent when someone is responding in an unusual manner. It could be a test to see how I react; whether I say something right or wrong. Prayer is the only way out of a mess, and God usually turns our mess into a message. When I feel weak, all I have left is prayer. Whether it is to cry and pray with all my strength or to meditate and listen to gospel music, I'll do what it takes to get my mind off myself and fix it on Him.

I would never encourage anyone to have a pity party of why things did not go to plan or why they think life isn't fair. This takes up too much time and energy. If you really want to see progress, start with gratitude and praise. Be thankful for all that you have and see it work out for your good. I can't stress how important words are to the mind. What you speak on will grow, so watch the seeds as you are watering them with your words.

Advice from the Father

I have been astonished by the thought that God desires to be known by His human creation.

We don't know what the next second brings, but God is graciously able to use any situation for good. This does not mean the paths He chooses will be easy; however, I choose to trust that His direction and timing are ultimately for my good. I believe that God wants us to be very intentional about the way we live. It is important to think about the legacy we leave on earth because every day we are writing it. Matthew 6:26 talks about the birds of the air, not being concerned about what they will eat or drink or where they will stay, knowing that God has kept a special place for them. God is known by His creation, the animals and stars He made, in reference to Genesis 1.

When I talk about advice from the Father, I am referring to God Almighty speaking. In Chapter 1, I explained about the Holy Spirit being the Comforter. God does not want us to worry about what has been taken away, however, he advises us to use our pain and turn it into purpose. His advice always comes from a place of peace, and not confusion.

When you really get to understand and give God a chance in your life, there will be situations and revelations that will start to make sense and realise why you had to go through so much in life. I am a living witness to the advice I receive not only from speaking to God but studying the Bible and praying fervently. It takes great worship, surrender, and sacrifice to give my undivided attention, but in the end, it always works for my good.

I am not here bragging about my perfect relationship with God, but I can say that through my flaws and mistakes, I've learnt to embrace and accept them for the better. When losing a special person, it is easy to take it out on anyone you see and then it becomes uncontrolled; it is likely that anything someone says will go in one ear and come out of the other. How could I have been the only person to understand God's love even after my sister's death? It is because He created a place for those who believe in Him, and even when we don't understand the circumstances that hit us, there is still the voice that speaks despite the depth of pain.

The truth is, no matter who we listen to, there is no one as loyal and trustworthy as God. We are incapable of carrying the load ourselves and have little control over the events of our lives, whether we view those events as favourable or not. This advice gave me inner peace because I don't control my life or make it the way I want it to be. Instead, I allow God to take over by renewing my mind and being positive. He reminds me that all things are made beautiful at the right time.

In seasons of heartache, trusting God is all I have - to bring a fresh perspective to what is given and the grace to endure. I may not always relish every season, but in the end, there is beauty that comes from it all. *God desires to use the hard times to develop perseverance and character and bring a satisfying hope-filled life.* Remember that advice God grants can't be equated to the advice given by people. There is a difference. When I want to make a decision, I make a conscious decision to seek God first (Matthew 6:33), so that I don't become confused and indecisive. When I feel difficulty becoming intense, I have to think back on the trials God brought me out from.

It is then I am able to remember the promises and peace He provides when I learn to take heed of the advice given and the ability for Him to sustain me. Isaiah 64:4 reads:

"Even to my old age, He will sustain and carry me"

I remember talking to my sister and saying how our appearances will look when we reach over 100 years! I pray to age gracefully with all my teeth intact and hair still full and thick! Yes, I will still dream when I am old! You should too! I remember sitting next to a lady in my church and she reminded me that when I get old, I should cherish and appreciate it. She was so happy and jolly. I will never forget her optimism!

No matter what age you leave the earth, remember to live a pleasant life so that people will remember you for great things. Do not take life into your own hands thinking it is all about you, because we are all important. The advice that comes from the Father can only be given when we fully surrender to Him. No matter what age or time God takes a loved one, His timing is best and He knows why. We should not try to understand or question His sovereignty but use departure to draw us closer to the Father, keeping us in perfect peace. Don't neglect hearing God's voice with yours. Yes, when you are in a difficult season, it is difficult to hear the Lord's voice, but with practise, time and patience it shall become easier. Learn to breathe in and breathe out.

The best advice is to have a God-awareness approach so that you can see His handiwork in every difficulty you encounter. A comforter advises and gives consolation in time of need. Glory and worry can't live in the same room. This is why God is in contrast to both seasons; good and bad, however in the end, the advice will always be sound and true. Allow Him to speak to your heart, be open-minded and listen. He wants to speak with you constantly.

My plans for you are unerring and will triumph as you trust the voice within which assures you (in spite of observed circumstances) that I cannot fail a trusting child. Give Me the glance of utter trusting love.

God can do more with our pain than we can ever imagine if we just trust in His love and heed His advice. When communicating with God, He is not harsh, but gentle. We have to practise discipline in listening when He speaks and be obedient to His word. This takes a lot of strength but with practise it does get better. I remember when studying the Word, I found it quite difficult to understand, particularly the Old Testament. Now, what I do is ask God for wisdom and understanding before opening the Bible, and it flows much better. There is no other comfort than the Holy Spirit and His Word. When I find trouble calling, the Word is what I turn to, because the promises He has uttered shall come to pass. I don't feel worried when studying the Word because everything I need to know is included. It completes me and helps me to take rest, rather than trying to do everything in my own power.

Each day is an opportunity to discipline our ears to hear what God says. This takes consistent practise, patience, and humility but it is worth it. We are able to know what direction to take simply because we have allowed Him to take the upper hand in our lives. I don't want to keep trying so hard to make things right when all I need is His approval. That is what gives me great pleasure, believing that those He desires to be in my life will come at the appointed time. I am not going to compromise what I know will benefit me in the long run till the end of time; rather I choose to make a decision and stand on God's promises, even when all feels like it is failing. There is reassurance and peace in the Bible which can't be negotiated. The promises of God are YES and AMEN! There is nothing that God does not understand about anyone; it just takes a willing person to surrender and listen to what He has to say.

I do not try to go my own way and make decisions that look good, but in the long run, will cause me to go back to where I started. Matthew 6:33 acknowledges God as a Father and ruler of everything. It reminds me that without Him, I can't do anything, because all power is in His Hands, and He has full control over life and death. I may be wise in my own eyes about the way I choose to live, but eventually, I end up surrendering because I want the peace that surpasses all human understanding. I don't want worldly or societal peace. I want the advice that comes from the Word and keeps me on my feet. I don't want to burn out trying to solve my own problems, when 1 Peter 5:7 encourages us to cast our burdens unto Him because He cares. Now, you have a decision to either solve your problems alone or give it to the One who sees the end from the beginning.

--- CHAPTER 8 ---
My Sister GLORY

Your life will never be the same – you are moving from Glory to Glory!

"My Child, Heaven is the place where you will finally find complete rest for your soul. Heaven is a guarded place, where I have the great joy of seeing My children kept from all false beckonings, and from every kind of danger. It is here that My children whom I have saved for Myself, share in what they have been anticipating. My child, do not be anxious about the hour at which you may eventually leave your earthly existence – simply look forward to the perfect understanding which awaits you"

Father John Woolley, 1984

"The Glory of this present house will be greater than the Glory of the former house, says the Lord Almighty"

Haggai 2:9 (NIV)

You can't change the past, but you can change what you do about your present. The word 'Glory' is powerful in itself. Earlier in the Introduction, I mentioned seven attributes that represent the word GLORY:

Power, Authority, Strength, Praise, Honour, Riches, and Respect

Glory is expensive, and nothing can surpass the beauty of its meaning. A song my dad loved to sing when we were young, says:

From Glory to Glory

"You are the Lord, that is your Name, You will never share your Glory with any man, You will never share your Glory with anybody, Almighty God, that is your Name"

Nigerian Praise

My sister, Glory, truly defines who she is; bold, wise, funny, bubbly, caring, and above all, humble. I could write a dissertation about her because only those that are close to my family know how she is. Even when I'm upstairs in my room, I can identify who was coming up the stairs, who was in the bathroom, and who was the last person to leave the house!

Glory is a diva; she loved going to The Body Shop for a free make over! She would come home and give us free goodies including nail vanishes, body sprays, perfumes, scarfs, to name a few.

When I plan events, she literally was my WHSmith! Pens, plastic wallets, permanent board markers were all with her!

She is one of a kind; very sharing (sharing is caring as she would mention) and wanted to make sure the family is always happy.

The following contributions are from the immediate family from my father, mother, sister, and brother:

<u>Justin Jacob (Father of Glory)</u>

Glory is always fun to be with and is a ray of sunshine to the family. There is never a dull moment in her life. Whatever she has, she shares with her family; birthdays, Father's Day, Christmas and wedding anniversaries. She is a blessing to the family financially, and a very bubbly woman.

She is always the first person to arrive at the altar to dance. Always looking after young children in the church. I remember on my 60th birthday where she told me that she'd make me a proud grandfather before death came calling. Although you did not fulfil this dream, I am still very proud of you as my beloved daughter.

Nothing in this world can erase your name from the Jacob family. Continue to rest in the bosom of our Lord and Saviour, Jesus Christ. We will meet in Heaven and part no more till eternity. I love you loads. Dad, Justin Jacob.

<u>Patience Jacob (Mother of Glory)</u>

Words are not enough for me to describe Glory my daughter, my first fruit from God. Glory has touched so many lives in tremendous ways because she is my daughter and I know what I am talking about.

Glory lived a life worth talking about as there was nothing that hindered her from what she wanted to do. She is as bold as a lion as she always stands her ground to threat and intimidation. She easily let go of her anger and annoyance just as the bible puts it "don't allow your anger to be with you until the sun goes down" (Ephesians 4:26).

I remember each time we are at the table for breakfast, lunch or dinner, we always watch music on YouTube which she plays for us as we enjoy our meals. There will never be another Glory in my family, but her legacy will live with us till eternity.

I remember on Thursday 27th December 2018, my husband and I went to the cemetery to visit her and met two ladies; their mothers' grave being next to my daughters. One of the ladies hugged and told me not to worry that her mother will look after Glory in Heaven. Even in her grave, Glory still has fans! Glory, I am very proud of you as a mother and what a name you have. There is never a time that your name, Glory, is not mentioned in songs, ministration, or the Word.

God Almighty chose that name for you because before you were born, God knew you (Jeremiah 1:5). You knew clearly where you were going as you mentioned from Monday 7th May, that you would be going home after five days. I remember telling you to wait for either Saturday or Sunday before going home. Keep dancing and praising God as this is what gave Him pleasure while you were here on earth.

I, your mother, miss you terribly much, but who am I to question the Almighty who has taken Glory for His Own Glory? Blessed be the Name of the Lord. Glory, my dear, till we meet again, may God Almighty grant you eternal rest. Love, Mum.

<u>Ruth Jacob (Sister of Glory)</u>

Glory was and always will be my loving big sister. The first sibling I ever knew, she always wanted to take care of me when we were younger. Her presence and personality would light up any room and her love for others was so evident, whether they were young or old. Her smile and laughter could catch anyone's attention and always brought a positive feeling to whoever was around.

Although my shared time with Glory at home was filled with laughing, music, watching TV, dancing and eating, our time together at primary school was short, due to the fact that she had moved on into secondary school by the time I got into the juniors playground. But I remember the times when we would walk to and from school each day.

There are so many qualities and principles that I learnt from her, such as being kind and generous to others and how what you sow can become what you reap. I remember those mornings when she would be getting ready for secondary school, I would make her break time snacks. Years later when she would attend her weekly cooking classes, the food that she made would be the meals that I'd take to work for my lunch!

I am also reminded of her generous heart. She would be the person to bring drinks for guests and also helped to supply the family with ample quantities whenever we attended parties!

Glory had a solid determination to live her best life and she didn't like being stuck indoors or in one place. She made the most of every opportunity to learn and live life to the fullest.

Her determination was even more present when she was admitted to hospital. Her faith and boldness inspired me to carry on, regardless of how many people speak against you and put you down. This is something that encourages me day by day and it shows that sometimes life's most painful lessons can be great experiences for training and developing your faith.

It happens to the best of us, but one thing I'm certain of is that I have a stronger determination because of the strength I saw in Glory. By divine conviction, she even knew when she was going home, and I rejoice because she's in a wonderful place and in the Heavenliest of surroundings. You will always be remembered and the positive impact that she imparted in the lives of so many will live on.

One thing I am certain of is that her memory will live on. Although you went away too soon, God sees and knows everything and I believe that at the right time the wrongs will be corrected and made right. We'll see you again, smiling and caring for others as you always did. Until then, and on this side of eternity, be sure to know you will not be forgotten and things will work out for good and for God's Glory.

I love you my dear big sis and will remember you always!

Remain richly blessed,

From your little sister,

Ruth xXx

Nathaniel-Faith Jacob (Brother of Glory)

Glory is power, strength, and respect in all things (to me anyway). She was and always will be my big sister who lived a carefree, positive and eventful life. She always got her way and did things her way. There was never a day where we didn't argue and I never 100% used to understand why she did certain things.

It only became clearer as of late 2017/early 2018 when she was still alive and when we coincidentally became closer. She will ride for you and be there for you no matter what. Always up for a laugh and always ready to cheer you up.

She is literally a positive spirit that is always with me and looks after me, forever blessing my going out and coming in. Despite our differences and frequent arguments, I wouldn't change that girl for anyone because she helped my family in so many ways imaginable. She is a guardian angel, a servant of God and most importantly, a friend. Rest in paradise my dearest love.

Until We Meet Again

The practice of daily gratitude can't erase the magnitude of pain we feel in seasons of loss.

Your Father in Heaven knows what is best for you. Of course, it is not easy losing a loved one and I did not realise how much it hit me until it came from my immediate family. When you hear about other people's stories about losing loved ones, you may not be able to understand however much you sympathise with them.

Now that it has happened, empathy is the closest action to take; whether you cry when one cries, it makes a big difference in ones' life. I can't imagine what Job in the Bible faced emotionally, spiritually and mentally when he lost his children. He did, however, say in Job 1:21:

"The Lord gave and has taken away; may the Name of the Lord be praised"

This could not have been easy to say, however, it signified his strength and trust in God who is the Comforter of our lives. Jesus is going to come in His Father's Glory with His angels and will reward each person according to what he has done (Matthew 16:27).

Apostle Paul also emphasised on this scripture:

"For me to live is Christ, and to die is gain"

Philippians 1:21

The time we have left on earth matters to God. My sister and I held Glory's hand at the side of the bed believing that God would keep her life. I then realised after the Lord took her the next day, it was a strong sign that God did not just create us to live and die on earth, but there is a much better place that He prepared for us (John 14:1-3).

From Glory to Glory

No matter how many accolades achieved or the amount of money we have, nothing in this life will fully satisfy. When a loved one departs, it is a time for self-reflection, to be sincere with and question what legacy you will leave.

The time we have left on earth matters to God because how we live is an indication of how people will view Him

I understand the importance of living an impactful life which inspires other people to see the best in themselves and recognise the worth they have. You are reading this book and you have a purpose. Do not disqualify yourself because of past mistakes or how society perceives you to be. As mentioned previously, a lot of young teenagers and adults in the UK have left way before their time. It is burdensome, but as we wake up each day, there is still a possibility that change will be made with the time left on earth.

This book is dedicated to those who lost someone in the past or recently – know that God is standing with you and can relate to all the feelings in the world you are experiencing right now. As your loved ones have gone with the Lord, your longing to join them will only increase. I keep saying that heaven is a beautiful place and I know Glory is looking down on me and my family ALWAYS! It has not been an easy road, but I'm assured that she is resting in eternal peace with no more pain and ache. If I could try to explain the pain my sister was feeling, I would not even know where to start. Glory really had a fighting, strong spirit – something that not a lot of people can survive, but yet, she still persevered.

I remember my mum speaking to me about a scripture just after Glory departed. It was in Psalm 90:12 which states:

"Teach us to number our days that we may gain a heart of wisdom"

As I will tell you, Glory, my sister, we surely will meet again. I know it will be a very long time till then, but for now, I am pressing on. I am working hard and doing everything to make sure impact is made. When people come and ask, 'How do you do it? How are you so strong and yet still smiling?' All I can tell them is: 'It's not by might, nor by power, but by my Spirit, says the Lord!' There is nothing I do in my own strength, especially when it comes to a sensitive topic including death.

My heart is deeply saddened by people who have not yet fully let go of the pain of their loved ones. I listen to them and give the time to allow the tears to flow. It really is okay to scream and shout, even when you want to try and remain calm. Rather than seeing your loved one as a loss, see it as an investment and addition to the Kingdom of God.

I know the enemy would have thought I'd be crumbling or pulling my hair out, but Glory didn't have that giving-up spirit, and that is what I have taken from her. She has imparted a lot of strength in me so why do I need to entertain emotional thoughts that are inconsistent? Glory, you are rejoicing now, and away from the pain.

You have taught me how to stand firm and be confident in who I am and not to allow anyone to take advantage. You went through so much, and yet you were still happy. You smiled and laughed through the pain.

I saw when you were always dancing despite the aches and uncomfortable moments. How can I not gain confidence in that? This is something I've had to discipline my mind with; to see beauty in pain and turn it into purpose. I wanted to see growth in this situation and I really did. If there is anything I'll take away from this is to use your story to inspire many people around the world, knowing that your departure will bring souls back to Christ. Don't take your life for granted, please.

I would have several dreams of Glory and made my mum and I would smile so much! At times the dreams felt SO REAL! I remember a dream where my mum and I were in her room and we were all so happy because Glory's bed was made. With her gorgeous laugh and big smile, the dream felt super real, until I woke up.

I started smiling in the end, because all the dreams about my sister have been amazing! It did, however, feel empty when my sister wasn't at the Christmas celebration 2018, however, we knew that her Spirit was with us. I often ask how people cope with having several years of Christmas holidays without their loved ones, and now I am able to look up to them more. It is really inspiring.

As we ponder the road ahead, may God give us wisdom and courage to follow His ways – the road of LIFE. It will make all the difference for us and those we love.

"But small is the gate and narrow the road that leads to life, and only a few find it"

Matthew 7:14 (NIV)

We will all meet our loved ones again, that I know for sure. Whether you have dreams of your loved ones, nothing will ever replace them. Their spirit still dwells within us. I know Glory will always be surrounded by us. She is a blessing to so many people and when we see her, she will be in a different dimension of Glory. I desire my readers to understand this book, coming from a very personal and transparent place.

God is real – He is love, and what is waiting for us when we leave the earth is far greater than earthly possessions. Yes, we will surely enjoy our lives here, but must also be conscious that:

our existence won't be forever

I am honoured to have a big sister like Glory who had such a big smile and wonderful soul, that when people saw her they knew that something was different. She will see us as the Jacob family and we shall see her. I encourage everyone who has lost or is still going through the grieving process to hold on. There is much more joy on the other side of life. ***Death is not the end.***

From Glory to Glory we are moving forward. Glory woke me up and made me realise that life truly is fleeting, so forgive quickly, love and learn to let go quickly, because it is one thing to not forgive and another thing to wake up and realise the person you once loved is no more. *We can't put a price on departure*.

God gives, and He takes; blessed be the Name of the Lord. His comfort is what assures us that we are in safe hands on earth and in Heaven. Stand strong in the midst of trials and know that the One who created you will come through.

Until we meet again, I stand firm on the promises of God. Many are out there still wondering why life is hard, but it will get better when God is in the centre of your heart.

At the appointed time, our lives will come to an end, but the end is just the beginning of a new eternal life. Don't wait to be serious when death comes, be serious now! Let your legacy leave a fresh aroma each day you wake up. Glory, keep resting in perfect peace; your presence will not be forgotten. You have given the family more strength. With love, now and always – the Jacob family.

Who would imagine losing something so precious unexpectedly? When you cherish something so deeply, you would not want anyone to take advantage of it. Glory is a gem, a precious woman who lived a free life.

The song that will always remind me of you, Glory, is *The Old Rugged Cross* by George Bennard, (1913).

From Glory to Glory

The words read:

On a hill far away, stood an old rugged Cross

The emblem of suffering and shame

And I love that old Cross where the dearest and best

For a world of lost sinners was slain

So I'll cherish the old rugged Cross

Till my trophies at last I lay down

I will cling to the old rugged Cross

And exchange it some day for a crown

Oh, that old rugged Cross so despised by the world

Has a wondrous attraction for me

For the dear Lamb of God, left his Glory above

To bear it to dark Calvary

So I'll cherish the old rugged Cross

Till my trophies at last I lay down

I will cling to the old rugged Cross

And exchange it some day for a crown

In the old rugged Cross, stain'd with blood so divine

A wondrous beauty I see

For the dear Lamb of God, left his Glory above

To pardon and sanctify me

150

So I'll cherish the old rugged Cross
Till my trophies at last I lay down
I will cling to the old rugged Cross
And exchange it some day for a crown

To the old rugged Cross, I will ever be true
Its shame and reproach gladly bear
Then He'll call me some day to my home far away
Where his Glory forever I'll share

So I'll cherish the old rugged Cross
Till my trophies at last I lay down
I will cling to the old rugged Cross
And exchange it some day for a crown.

--- The Funeral of Glory Jacob ---
Jacob's Family Tributes

Father and Mother's Tribute to Glory Jacob

We are very privileged to have you, Glory, born into the Jacob family. Unquestionable God - that is who our God is to us. You will always be in our hearts and dreams. Glory was ill at work where she was taken to Lewisham hospital by the staff of Lewisham Nexus.

We never knew the severity of the sickness until a few weeks later where she was diagnosed with ovarian cancer. Glory never complained or stressed anyone with anything around her. Glory stayed in Lewisham hospital for four weeks and three days before being transferred to St Thomas's hospital.

Glory had her operation on Tuesday 10th April 2018. The doctors told us that the operation was successful, and we were sent home after one week. Only to our surprise that her tummy grew back to the same as it were before. We were re-admitted to St Thomas' Hospital for the second time where the doctor told us that Glory cannot make it due to the aggressiveness of the cancer. We remember after the doctor told us when we came to the room that Glory said to her mum and dad, 'if the doctors haven't got anything nice to say, they should keep it to themselves'.

I remember when Glory stood up from her chair and hugged me and then sat down; a second time, she stood up again and hugged me tightly to my surprise; it was as if she was saying her final goodbyes. We will never forget your words when you all tell us that: 'sharing is caring'. You did not leave your strong faith with you as you always say, that once you feel better, you will be coming back to the church to dance.

You always had a positive attitude towards everything. I remember when the staff at Lewisham Nexus called in to cheer you up and informed them that you were getting better little by little. We remember when the church had Higher Praise Concert in 2018 where you were very upset that you did not attend, but mum told you that there will be many more years to come and she mentioned that the next year Higher Praise Concert 2019 will not be missed.

During Dad's 60th birthday in 2016, Glory gave a speech that she was going to make her family proud where she will get married and have her own children. Glory had high hopes, and nothing could put her down. I could remember as soon as you open the door, all we could hear is 'hello hello hello, how is everybody doing?' And you would zoom straight to your room!

You always said to mum 'please don't make yellow food too late' (that is pounded yam by the way). We cannot forget when at the dining table, you would play gospel music on YouTube while we were eating dinner. You had everything going for you until death came calling. Glory, you were loved by those around you. You have affected so many lives with your love, especially at Sureway church. There was never any dull moment in your life.

Your family in Nigeria misses you, and as you told my brother that you will be coming home in December 2018 to see them, you made a list of all the things that you will do when you get there. We will always be reminded of your positive thoughts.

Glory will never be forgotten in the life of the Jacob family because some of the things you did are amazing, and you have left an indelible mark in our hearts. We will miss you as God has taken to you Glory for His own Glory. Rest in eternal Peace in Jesus Name, Amen.

From Glory to Glory

Ruth Jacob's Tribute to Glory Jacob

Glory you were my big sister. My earliest memories of you involved us having to stay awake for what felt like an eternity every morning, before leaving for primary school.

We had to be awake and dressed by mum at 06:30am, having to wait until about 08:30am before heading off to school. Now, for two young children, staying in one place for two hours really feels like an eternity and the only way we could pass away time was by watching TV.

But mum would always turn the TV off from the socket, so I would end up crying out of boredom. Each time, you knew exactly what to do and would turn the TV on from the plug and then I would calm down.

This was one of my first tastes of journalism and I truly believe that times like these were what shaped my interest in this as a future career. Being around you sis helped me to realise what my interests were, and you inadvertently helped to shape a key interest for my future.

I remember how I would buy magazines and you would flick through them, or anytime I came in with a new bag, you would whip it straight on and catwalk around the house saying, 'check me out!'

Your personality and character would fill the house. At dinner time you would play Gospel on YouTube and tapping away your hopes and aspirations for the future. You loved to cook and took part in weekly classes, where your Wednesday meals would be my Thursday lunch!

Some of your greatest qualities, have been told by the people who saw you work, especially mothers who have told of how you impacted their children's lives; making sure they had snacks and food to eat and they were cared for and not crying. This is exactly what you did for me all those years ago when we were growing up.

I remember your speech at Dad's 60th birthday where you told us all the wonderful things on your heart and I can say that your words will not fall to the ground sis.

I may not be able to share precious moments with you. I'll never be able to boop you again or call you Glory Yakatori, or see your love hearts in our cards, or the three musketeers!!! But I am glad that you're resting and no more in pain from this wicked and cruel world.

Your Christian faith and passionate desire to be in church – singing, dancing, serving and being joyful in the presence of God have encouraged me to grow closer to the LORD and desire to develop healthy, genuine and strong relationships in the church.

I'm glad to say this is still going on and I'm moving forwards because of the strength of character I've seen in you and will keep on working until it's my own time to go. God bless you sis; rest in the LORD and we shall see each other again one day.

Heaven was your hope, now heaven is your home.

Rest in your Saviour's love and we will see you again one day and then for eternity in Christ.

From Glory to Glory

Esther Jacob's Tribute to Glory Jacob

No-one knows tomorrow. I would not have ever imagined myself sharing this. There are simply no words to describe the way I feel at this moment in time. But what I can confidently say is GOD IS FAITHFUL! I've learnt that God gives, and God takes away. He is perfect in all of His ways because He is a good, good Father.

My sister, Glory was a unique individual; a free woman and spirit that enjoyed her independence.

She always fed me when I was young and consistently dropped me off at school. As I was going through the picture album, I realised how long her hair was. Longer than Brazilian and Peruvian hair women wear today – she was distinctive. No one could really understand the unique abilities she had apart from my family. Her smile can light up a dark room alongside her laugh. She made a big difference to those around her without realising. She was strong – boy, if you mess with her, it is a rap for you!

Her unique ability to relate to the young children was contagious, her work colleagues and family.

I still remember my dad in hospital asking her when she would like to go home. She mentioned Friday! My dad said, "why not Saturday?", but she insisted Friday as she wanted to watch TV in her room. We were rest assured that, indeed, Friday would be the day she would come home with us. When Thursday evening came, Glory got up from her chair and hugged my dad twice.

It was as if she was saying her last goodbyes before departing. The Holy Spirit must have informed Glory in advance that He is ready to take her. We thought she was coming back home, but God took her to His Kingdom.

Low and behold, Friday came, and there she was, still – with the angels ministering to her soul. Specifically, at 07.00am in the morning, Glory was passed on to Glory – my mother witnessed it all.

But guess what? Do you know what the number 7 represents? It represents 'completion' – this indeed was the Will of God for her to depart on the day she wanted.

No more pain, no more agony, no more tears, no more sorrow. I will never forget the hugs and kisses she gave us every time my family would visit her. She would always do her 'queens wave' and escort us out of the hospital. When I say my sister is one of a kind, she really is. Through her passing on, I have learnt to enjoy my life even more.

The blessings hidden behind her departure can now unravel. This is not a time to cry, but a time to rejoice, knowing that one day we shall see her again. My family can gently move on with grace, knowing that she has left a strong legacy on the earth. Her name alone can fight any demon or situation – she really was and will always be a blessing to us. Be reminded that death is not the end, but just the beginning of an everlasting eternal journey.

If it could be my will, I would have wanted her to attend my future wedding and meet my husband and children. But regardless, God is still God – and nothing can separate the love between us (Romans 8:28). Indeed, she was ready to leave this world, full of pain and sorrow. She is now in eternal peace resting in the heavenly realms watching down on us, smiling, dancing, relaxing. Nothing can and will ever replace my big sister, she is expensive and authentic.

God can take anyone He wants without questioning His sovereignty. So I am here to remind you – *The Lord is coming soon, are you ready?* I know she was!

From Glory to Glory

Nathaniel-Faith Jacob's Tribute to Glory Jacob

A message to my eldest sister: Thank you for being a part of my life. Glory, you are and always will be such a strong individual. Life hasn't been the same since you left and it's so crazy that I woke up at 07.00am on Friday 11th May and you sadly passed on at 07.00am. We had countless arguments but regardless, I still respected you as my big sister. It's a shame that you couldn't physically see the glow up, but I know for a fact that you are watching from Heaven.

Ever since you left, I feel there has been a gap in the family, like something is missing. I'll never forget the way I celebrated you on your 35th birthday without you being here. It literally felt like my whole world was ending and sleeping was more difficult than it already was. Going to see you on your birthday and tying the birthday balloon to your grave reminded me of Romans 8:38-39 – nothing and absolutely nothing will separate us from the love of Christ.

Regardless of you not being here in person, your spirit and happiness will always reside within me and my household. The same blessings that you received when you went out and always came home safely, are the same blessings that I am receiving right now – forever blessing my going out and my coming in.

You will be in my heart and mind for the rest of my days, my dearest love. Rest in paradise, much love.

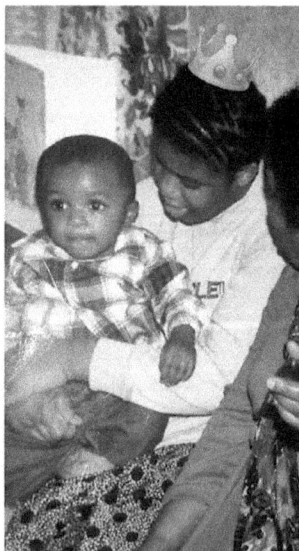

--- Glory Chidinma Jacob ---

Glory Chidinma Jacob was born on Monday 26th September 1983 in Lagos, Nigeria, to Mr Justin and Mrs Patience Jacob. By the age of 3, she moved to the UK with her family. She attended Monson Primary School, Hundson Road, in New Cross. After her primary school education, Glory went to Pendragon Secondary School (now Drumbit, in Bromley). She proceeded to Lewisham College where she studied floral arrangement.

Glory was someone who loved learning, even after her college education, she would attend courses in a range of subjects from IT to Catering. Glory was employed by Lewisham Nexus as an Administrator and Receptionist and had worked for the company for over 15 years until her passing on to Glory on Friday 11th May 2018 at 07.00am in the arms of her mother.

Glory worked in Sureway's ushering and children's department; she enjoyed helping the children's ministry and looking after them. She worked with great energy and passion. She loved to dance in the church as well.

Glory, you came, you saw, and you conquered. But above all, you died in the Lord and your death is not in vain. Glory left behind two sisters, Ruth and Esther and her little brother, Nathaniel-Faith Jacob. Though you are gone, you will never be forgotten. We love you Glory, but Jesus loves you most.

Rahin Ohuma Ime Efa Jesus Christ **(Agbor Dialect)**

Translation: Sleep well in Jesus Name

From Glory to Glory

A song by Hillsong (Broken Vessels) dedicated to you, Glory:

All these pieces, broken and scattered
In mercy gathered, mended and whole
Empty-handed, but not forsaken
I've been set free, I've been set free

Amazing grace, how sweet the sound, that saved a wretch like me,
oh
I once was lost, but now I'm found, was blind but now I see
Oh, I can see it now, oh, I can see the love in Your eyes
Laying yourself down, raising up the broken to life.

You take our failure, you take our weakness
You set Your treasure, in jars of clay
So take this heart, Lord, I'll be Your vessel
The world to see, your life in me, oh

Amazing grace, how sweet the sound, that saved a wretch like me,
oh
I once was lost, but now I'm found, was blind but now I see
Oh, I can see it now
Oh, I can see the love in Your eyes
Laying yourself down
Raising up the broken to life.

--- CHAPTER 9 ---
My Closing Thoughts

The Ultimate Destiny

Every one of us grows closer to the day of death with each and every passing breath

There is a purpose far greater than material prosperity and is held securely by the One who never leaves and never forsakes us. The greatest in the Kingdom of God are not those who are served BY the largest number, but those who serve THE largest number. The ultimate destiny we must consider is where we shall be going when passing on.

It is not usually a question that people may want to talk about, because yes, of course, we do want to have a fulfilled and plentiful life here. I remember when studying the book of Revelation, it reminds us that we will give an account to God on judgment day. No matter how many awards or recognition, what will I gain from them if I have not fulfilled my ultimate purpose?

We all have a role to actively partake in. You may know your purpose and you may not. At some point, it will be revealed to you. If you have a burden for homeless people or an empathetic heart towards grievance and loss, there are words of encouragement from the Bible that can lift the pain. You can use this as an indication to what you have been called to do. What frustrates you, you have the ability to change when you put your mind to it.

We have to get to a point where we start speaking life into situations even when it does not seem anything is changing. I have understood that through my destiny, is attached many struggles, detours, and frustrations, but in the end, they all work out for my utmost good, to help me regain strength and impact other people.

From Glory to Glory

Struggle is always pregnant with Glory

Through Glory's departure, it won't always be easy for one to understand the process because how can one question departure? It just happens. *My sister's departure is a real opportunity to invite others to know Jesus.* I always have at the back of my mind that I may not always see results when telling someone about Jesus in the midst of loss, but humbled to share this with them. I love being vulnerable as it shows strength and meekness at the same time. It is my role to speak about it, allowing the Holy Spirit to take over. Our destiny is about being able to live for God and doing good to everyone we meet. You may only get one opportunity to meet someone, so be kind.

Jesus trusted in God when He was in an intense time of being nailed to the cross. He approached His own death and prayed for strength. Because of Jesus, there is full confidence that whatever we face, God is with us, rest assured of that. This is what I continue to hold on to, especially when death comes knocking. God used death to strengthen my faith so when greater trials come, I can sing with confidence about His love. David, when he was being afflicted by King Saul states in Psalm 116:10:

"I trusted in the Lord when I said: "I am greatly distressed"

It takes deep strength to trust God even when one is in anguish. There is a tendency to grit teeth and question why things are always going wrong, but there is a lesson to learn from it and to stand firm to trust God which is a sign of great faith and reward. If David made it through, surely you can too, even when you think it isn't possible.

Despite the trials and even unexpected death, we can still have confidence in God's love. I can say that 2018 has been a year of raw testing of faith. Notwithstanding, I choose to see life as a journey and eventually end to the final destination, which is Heaven. John 14:1-3 reminds us not to allow our hearts to be troubled as we believe in God. In His house are many mansions and He is already preparing a place for us to stay.

Pondering on Revelation 19:6-7 it says:

"Then I heard what sounded like a great multitude, like the roar of rushing waters and loud peals of thunder shouting 'Hallelujah! For our Lord God Almighty reigns (7) Let us rejoice and be glad and give Him Glory'"

In all circumstances, we ought to give Him Glory. I was listening to a sermon from TD Jakes called "hearing when you are hurting". When I say this message hit home, it really did! He spoke on the story about Joseph in Genesis 37; when Joseph felt betrayed by his brothers who sold him into slavery, it caused him pain that could not be understood. At times, if I am honest, the pain speaks louder than wanting to forgive those who have hurt you. It takes an honest heart to surrender.

In the same sermon, TD Jakes also spoke about the process we go through when we are in a predicament. We *'buffer'*, meaning we subconsciously worry without realising the mental effects it has on our attitude, character, and well-being. We tend to control every aspect of our lives until we burn out and this isn't good for our health.

My destiny is not controlled by how I feel or what I want to see happen, but how God can entrust me with the gifts given. I remember walking home on a Friday afternoon in December and saw a young beautiful woman, aged around nineteen to twenty. Her hands were in her pockets and she looked down. As I was walking, I gently approached and told her about the love of Jesus. Whether she was a believer or not, I reassured her that what she was facing was preparing her for a better tomorrow and that it would make her much stronger. She understood every word that came out my mouth. She *listened* as I spoke. *It was the last Friday in 2018* and we spoke for around a minute. I gave her a hug in the end and could tell she was inspired; it was as if she needed the reassurance (which we all do from time to time). I left with tears because I never knew I'd walk up and start speaking a young lady.

From Glory to Glory

Servitude is the most selfless and humbling traits that are highly attractive. If I could have this opportunity again, I truly would do it! In my heart, I felt very happy. Whether you may be a believer or not, God's love is available to all, no matter your circumstance or past failure. I use my life as a living testimony to share my story and inspire people to use their obstacles as an opportunity to break free. What if I had walked past the woman without having a chance to speak? Destiny is not just about you, but the lives of others.

My sister Glory did not leave this earth for the family to mourn; she left to remind us of our purpose – that we have a job to fulfil before leaving. She reminded me to keep the fire burning within; to have the heart of love, warmth, and understanding towards those I meet. Even smiling is a sign of acceptance. *People have to see kindness in you before they see Jesus*. If there is no love in words, actions or deeds, how will people be convinced?

As we continue in life, what words are you going to leave behind for those who are still mourning? How can we support those who are in desperate need to move on? And how would you like people to remember you? No matter what, positive words go a long way than having a harbouring heart. 'I'm sorry' and 'thank you' can really be the best words someone needs to hear. Don't wait until it's too late. Each day matters and you are carrying the reputation of yourself all the time. Be intentional about your life and live it on purpose, with dignity and humility because you don't know who may be watching and being inspired. Your life matters so use it wisely. You are here for a reason. Make your presence known, felt and remembered.

"But we all, with unveiled face, beholding as in a mirror the Glory of the Lord, are being transformed into the same image from Glory to Glory, just as by the Spirit of the Lord"

2 Corinthians 3:18 (NKJV)

Paul sums up the Christian life, from redemption and sanctification on earth to our glorious eternal welcome into Heaven. There is a transition from one Glory to greater Glory; both having astonishing splendour. Paul presents one more astonishing claim:

"Therefore, if anyone is in Christ, he is a new creation; the old has gone, the new has come!"

2 Corinthians 5:17 (NIV)

This is an invitation the Lord makes to all of us to have our lives radically transformed here and now, by opening our eyes to see the glorious journey He is taking us on *from Glory to GLORY!*

Contacting the Author

Website Blog: www.womansworthconference.wordpress.com

Facebook Page: Women's Worth Conference

Website: www.authenticworth.com

Email: authenticworth@gmail.com

Instagram: authenticworth

Facebook Page: Authentic Worth

Personal Facebook: Esther Jacob

Personal Instagram: esthernjacob

Twitter: esthernjacob

YouTube: Esther N J

Speaking engagements: authenticworth@gmail.com

--- <u>REFERENCES</u> ---

Altucher:- UCBwordforyou
https://www.ucb.co.uk/content/comparison-trap-2 13th (September 2018)

Arnold, C:- Why Forgive, Orbis Books, 2010

Bevere, J:- The Bait of Satan: Living Free From the Deadly Trap of Offense, Charisma House, 2013

Bryan, J:- Living with Downs Syndrome, Wayland, 2006

Bryan, J:- I have Downs Syndrome, Gareth Stevens, 2010

Carruthers:- Esther Through the Centuries: Blackwell Bible Commentaries, Blackwell, 2007

Jakes, T:- Soar!, Little, Brown & Company, 2016

Jakes, T:- Hearing when you are hurting, TD Jakes, Dec 2018

Martin, J:- https://libquotes.com/josé-de-san-mart%C3%ADn/quote/lbe0t9c (La vida blanca (1960) by Eduardo Mallea, p.154)

Obama:- Becoming, Penguin Viking, 2018

Piper, J:- https://www.pinterest.com/colossians3vs1/john-piper/
Robertson, F.W:- http://scriptoriumdaily.com/f-w-robertsons-life-and-death/ (15th August 2010)

Roper, D:- Our Daily Bread 18 December 2018 Devotional – The Great Awakening

Savaloy, P., & Mayer, J:- What is emotional intelligence?
https://www.verywellmind.com/what-is-emotional-intelligence-2795423. (Sept 24th 2018).

From Glory to Glory

Shirer, P:- Discerning the Voice of God, 2007,
https://www.amazon.co.uk/Discerning-Voice-God-Recognize-
Speaks/dp/0802450091/ref=sr_1_3?ie=UTF8&qid=1550607593&sr=
8-3&keywords=discerning+the+voice+of+god+priscilla+shirer

Syed, M:- Bounce: The Myth of Talent and the Power of Practice,
2010. Link:
https://www.amazon.co.uk/Bounce-Myth-Talent-Power-Practice-
ebook/dp/B003P2WJ18

Woolley, J:- Many Mansions, Fr. John Woolley, 1984

NOTES

_____

_____

_____

_____

_____

_____

_____

_____

_____

_____

_____

_____

NOTES

_____

_____

_____

_____

_____

_____

_____

_____

_____

_____

_____

_____

_____

_____

www.ingramcontent.com/pod-product-compliance
Lightning Source LLC
Chambersburg PA
CBHW060336030426
42336CB00011B/1366